ART AT AUCTION 1979-80

PABLO PICASSO
Saltimbanque assis, les bras croisés
Signed and dated *23*, 51$\frac{3}{8}$in by 38$\frac{1}{4}$in (130.5cm by 97cm)
New York $3,000,000(£1,276,596). 12.V.80
From the collection of the late Edgar William and Bernice Chrysler Garbisch; now in the
Bridgestone Museum of Modern Art, Tokyo

ART AT AUCTION
The year at Sotheby Parke Bernet 1979-80

Two hundred and forty-sixth season

SOTHEBY PARKE BERNET

First published for
Sotheby Parke Bernet Publications by
Philip Wilson Publishers Ltd,
Russell Chambers, Covent Garden, London WC2E 8AA
and 81 Adams Drive, Totowa, New Jersey 07512

ISBN 0 85667 101 0
ISSN 0084-6783

Editor: Joan A. Speers
Assistant editor: Georgia Fogg
Assistants (USA): Betsy Pinover, Holly Williams
Production: Peter Ling, Harry Tyler, Mary Osborne

Distributed exclusively to the book trade in Germany,
Austria and Switzerland by Sotheby/Klett-Cotta, Stuttgart
(ISBN 3 8213 1002 2)

Printed in England by Jolly & Barber Ltd, Rugby

The publishers would like to acknowledge the National Gallery,
London, for their kind permission to reproduce the illustration
on p 21

Endpaper illustration: A repeating pattern from a design for a
decorative panel by Léon Bakst, sold in London on 13 March
1980 for £600 ($1,410)

Contents

An appliqued chintz and trapunto American eagle quilt, dated *1837*, probably New England,
8ft 10in by 8ft 10in (269cm by 269cm)
New York $7,500(£3,191). 2.II.80
From the collection of the late Priscilla A. B. Henderson

A wrought iron tabernacle door, French or Netherlandish, late fifteenth century, height $16\frac{1}{2}$in (42cm)
Zurich SFr 26,000 (£6,667 : $15,667). 7.V.80

Note

Prices given throughout this book are the hammer prices exclusive of any buyer's premium or sales tax which may have been applicable in any of the salerooms. These prices are shown in the currency in which they were realised. The sterling and dollar equivalent figures, shown in brackets, are for guidance only and are based on the rounded rates of exchange on 30 May 1980. These rates, for each pound sterling, are as follows:

United States dollars, 2.35; Canadian dollars, 2.70; Hong Kong dollars, 11.50; French francs, 9.70; Swiss francs, 3.90; Dutch guilders, 4.55; Italian lire, 1,964; South African rand, 1.80

Sotheby Parke Bernet's two main galleries, in Great Britain and the United States, are indicated by the designation 'London' or 'New York'. Additional salerooms in these two cities are referred to as 'Belgravia' and 'Hodgson's Rooms' (London) and 'PB Eighty-Four' (New York)

Fig 1
A sketch of Peter Wilson by Julian Barrow, made in 1978 for the oil painting presented to him by his fellow directors. PCW is auctioning the *armilla*, a twelfth-century enamel arm ornament, from the Robert von Hirsch Collection in the main Bond Street gallery, on 22 June 1978

PCW: auctioneer extraordinary

Frank Herrmann

On the evening of 15 October 1958 Peter Wilson, in evening dress, climbed into the rostrum of the main gallery at Bond Street, the glare of banked television lamps upon him. Fourteen hundred people had been allocated tickets for the occasion. They included Somerset Maugham, Anthony Quinn, Margot Fonteyn, Kirk Douglas, Lady Churchill and a great multitude of collectors and art dealers from all over the world. Two hours before the sale began the police had to be called to control the mass of people who wanted to gain admission. Only seven items were to be sold: three paintings by Manet; two by Cézanne; one by van Gogh and one by Renoir – all from the collection of the late Jakob Goldschmidt of New York.

It was the first occasion on which Sotheby's had held an evening sale since the eighteenth century. Preparations had been long and dramatic. The climax of the sale itself arrived with lot 6, Cézanne's *Garçon au gilet rouge* (Fig 2), which that night must have become one of the most photographed paintings in the world. Its subtle red tones looked superb against the greens and browns of the huge Brussels tapestry, used as a backdrop behind the rostrum. The bidding started at £20,000 and had within minutes risen to £200,000, then £220,000. That figure was by a great margin the highest price ever offered at auction for a work of art anywhere in the world. Peter Wilson intoned, '£220,000. What, will no one bid any more?' His tone of voice was that of a man genuinely astonished that a group of buyers of such distinction could let a painting of this quality go for so paltry a sum. A roar of laughter relieved the tension. The hammer came down. There was a momentary pause while people took in the significance of what they had just witnessed. Loud applause followed.

The Goldschmidt sale raised £781,000 in twenty-one minutes. It represented a major breakthrough in establishing London as the centre of the international art market. It was also based on an ingenious, albeit risky commission arrangement which required a good deal of nerve and confidence if it was to be profitable for Sotheby's – two qualities with which 'PCW' was blessed in abundance. In the event, the high total brought assured success. From that point onwards, property came to the firm for sale from all over the world in unprecedented quantities.

Thirty years of arduous training had prepared Peter Wilson for that moment: Eton, Oxford (briefly), a spell at Reuter's, another on the staff of the *Connoisseur*, acceptance by Sotheby's as a trainee in the furniture department in 1936, the first major sale he organised himself – that of the Edouard Gilhou Collection of antique rings in

November 1937 – where, after producing an unusually scholarly catalogue he was able to put to use a gift for stimulating wide public interest. During those early years, close family friendships with connoisseurs such as Margaret Jourdain, the authority on English furniture, Joan Evans, the antiquarian, Ralph Edwards, Keeper of Furniture at the Victoria and Albert Museum, and Dr Philip Nelson, the medievalist, helped to kindle his interest in detailed research and, above all, to train his eye in the appreciation of quality. He became a partner in the firm just before the war. Then followed five years of wartime service in Intelligence, much of it in America.

On his return to Bond Street in 1946 Peter Wilson at first looked after the works of art department, as well as being responsible for the appointment of new staff, a task which the older partners regarded as particularly important. In 1948 he switched roles and took charge of the picture department. Over a period of ten years, in association with Hans and Carmen Gronau, that department played an increasingly dominant role in the firm. Initially, oppressive government restrictions on free trade between Britain and countries overseas impeded progress, but in the early 1950s when revised legislation permitted the free flow of goods and money both in and out of the country, and the art market became increasingly international, the painting department flourished. Originally, there had been a concentration on the works of the old masters, but gradually it also became possible to foster within the auction room a growing interest in the works of the Impressionists and their followers. The William Weinberg sale in 1957 – the first of its kind to come to London from New York – had shown the way. Goldschmidt was the breakthrough.

But success had to be fought for. Competition for major sales increased, not only on home ground, but also from overseas. It revealed the quality of determination in PCW's make-up, which his gentle manner and unfailing courtesy concealed. A rival auctioneer, Maurice Rheims, remembers that fixity of purpose particularly well. He and PCW were to compete on many occasions. The first was over the sale of King Farouk's extraordinary collections in 1954. As soon as he heard of the royal abdication, PCW flew to Cairo to negotiate with the new revolutionary government. Rheims arrived rather later and managed to effect a compromise under which the French auctioneers were to collaborate with Sotheby's. Looking back on these events years later Maurice Rheims has recently written: 'Everything went off beautifully . . . But, alas! I had trodden on the cat's tail and Peter Wilson is no neutered pet but a formidable tom . . . He was to make me pay dearly for my audacity. In less than a decade he reversed the position, threw a blockade round Paris and made London the turntable of the art market'. Among subsequent battles were those over the collection of René Fribourg in New York in 1963, the acquisition of Parke-Bernet in 1964 and the opening of Sotheby's offices in Monte Carlo in 1975 with the sale of magnificent items from the collections of Baron Guy de Rothschild and Baron de Redé. There were no more compromises: Peter Wilson and Sotheby's were more than happy to go it alone.

Shortly after the Goldschmidt sale, PCW became Sotheby's chairman, following Vere Pilkington. During his first year in that role, Bond Street sold property worth more than £5,750,000, at that time the highest total ever achieved by a fine art auction house, and as the firm's *Annual Review* proudly stated 'virtually double that of any

Fig 2
Garçon au gilet rouge by Paul Cézanne, from the Jakob Goldschmidt Collection, sold in London on
15 October 1958 for £220,000

other in the world'. The decade that followed was probably the most momentous and exciting in the firm's long history. Not only was the quality of what was sold remarkable and the volume of important sales increasing, but the name of Sotheby's became familiar all over the world. PCW's vision of a genuinely international organisation slowly became a reality as more and more offices were opened abroad. The most important event by far in this outward expansion was the merger with Parke-Bernet in New York in August 1964, after protracted and infinitely complex negotiations. Like many other matters decided during this period, the original acquisition represented considerable commercial hazards. But PCW exuded a spirit of confidence and, backed by like-minded and incredibly hard-working colleagues, the risks taken usually justified themselves.

PCW's marvellous gift for engendering enthusiasm has been a major factor during his two decades of chairmanship in motivating his colleagues and staff. It has proved of equal importance in his friendship with many of the world's great collectors. His advice is eagerly sought, even when the acquisitions or disposals have nothing to do with Sotheby's. He has a deft touch, too, for diplomatic communication. When he visited Somerset Maugham on the Riviera to discuss the sale of his collection of Impressionists, there was no mention of the pictures until PCW was on the point of leaving. Only then did he raise the subject: 'The sale, is it to be June or October?' Or when he was asked by the *New York Times* whether Sotheby's got the Fribourg sale because the firm's commission rate was lower than that of its competitors, he commented, 'If you went to one doctor who said his fee was $100, another who said it was $50 and a third it was $10, you would not necessarily go to the $10 man. You'd go to the one you thought would cure you'.

In November 1979 at the age of sixty-six, PCW announced his intention to step down as chairman. He has moved to his house in Clavary in the south of France where, unlike some latter-day Cincinnatus, who might devote himself to art collecting, writing his memoirs or tending his favourite eucalyptuses, he will continue working for the firm in the generation of international business. Sotheby's has been the whole of his life: there is still much that he can contribute. He said farewell to his colleagues within the firm with a memorable and magnificent party at Leeds Castle.

Bond Street will seem different without PCW's tall, elegant, powerful frame strolling about the galleries. There are many who will miss the style he has made his own in the rostrum at major sales (Fig 1): the pregnant gesture, the momentary pause, the head tilted left and the come-on smile, the raised eyebrow, the deprecatory look that says 'you really should have made another bid', or that instant communication with a hesitant bidder that generates confidence, and the slow cadence of the falling gavel that gives competing buyers every chance to come in with another bid.

In the twenty-two years of his chairmanship PCW has given Sotheby's a new identity. In addition to increasing sales in a single year to thirty times what they had been in 1958, he has brought a fresh dynamic to the world of auctioneering that has helped to stimulate a degree of interest in the arts and in collecting, which former generations never dreamed of. Yet he has maintained in each of Sotheby's overseas centres concern for the individual client, the importance of expert knowledge and the dignity and integrity for which the firm has always been renowned.

Paintings and Drawings

MARIOTTO DI NARDO
The Nativity and *The Circumcision*
A pair, on panel, each 17in by 6¾in (43cm by 17cm)
London £44,000 ($103,400). 16.IV.80

This pair of paintings belongs to a series of panels of the life of Christ by Mariotto di Nardo

NICCOLO DI PIETRO GERINI
Christ on the Cross
On panel, 11in by 31¾in (28cm by 80.5cm)
London £38,000 ($89,300). 16.IV.80

HENDRIK GOLTZIUS
A vision of Christ crucified
On panel, signed and dated *AℓH.G.10* (1610), 37in by 25¾in (94cm by 65.5cm)
London £29,000 ($68,150). 16.IV.80

Fig 1
DIERIC BOUTS
The Resurrection
Tempera on cotton, mid fifteenth century, 35in by 28½in (89cm by 72.5cm)
London £1,700,000 ($3,995,000). 16.IV.80

Now in the Norton Simon Museum, Pasadena

Dieric Bouts – a Resurrection

Catherine Reynolds

The *Resurrection* attributed to Dieric Bouts (Fig 1) shows convincing stylistic similarities with the *Sacrament Altarpiece*, one of Bouts's two documented works. That the *Resurrection* is painted on cloth had led (even when known only from photographs) to its association with two other cloth paintings attributed to Bouts – an *Entombment* (Fig 2) in the National Gallery, London, and a *Crucifixion* in the Musées Royaux des Beaux-Arts, Brussels. Although documentary references imply that pictures on cloth were popular, being cheap and easily portable, their fragility means that few have survived from the early fifteenth century. The preservation of three from the same hand suggests a possible shared history, a theory which can be strongly supported for the *Resurrection* and the *Entombment* and not contradicted for the *Crucifixion*.

The *Entombment* and the *Resurrection* are practically the same size and both have a strip of fresher colour visible on the top and right edges, and to some extent on the left, showing that both had once been fixed to smaller stretchers before being restretched, thereby exposing the unfaded paint. It is highly improbable that the two pictures could independently have received identical treatment.

The *Entombment* was first recorded in notes of 1858 and 1860 by Sir Charles Eastlake, who bought the painting for the National Gallery. Originally owned by the Foscari, it was being sold by the Guicciardi family of Milan, who had acquired it in Vienna early in the century. In 1858, Eastlake mentions three other pictures with the *Entombment* – an *Adoration of the Kings*, a *Presentation* and an *Annunciation*. In 1860, he lists a *Crucifixion* instead of the *Presentation*. The omission of the *Resurrection* is inconclusive for Eastlake actually saw only the *Adoration* and the *Entombment*, which he called a *Descent from the Cross*. It has been proposed that, while accepting the same earlier provenance as the *Entombment*, the *Resurrection* was in Milan until the end of the nineteenth century, but it is unclear whether this idea is based on independent evidence or deduction. The *Crucifixion* cannot be traced definitely beyond the English abbey which sold it in 1928, but it is possible that it was bought in Italy in 1845, before Eastlake's visit. Unfortunately, the poor condition of this painting makes stylistic arguments even more tentative than usual.

However, if it is accepted that the three pictures belong together, some suggestions about their original arrangement can be made. The *Crucifixion* ($70\frac{1}{2}$in by $59\frac{7}{8}$in) is almost exactly double the size of each of the others, indicating an altarpiece like Bouts's *Sacrament Altarpiece*, where two smaller panels are placed one above the other on either side of the central panel – a reconstruction proposed by F. Winkler in an article in *Kunstchronik*, 1958. Of the subjects mentioned by Eastlake, the *Adoration* has some prophetic relevance to Christ's burial, and if the *Presentation* were actually a *Circumcision* (two events often confused) it would relate to the *Crucifixion* as the first shedding of Christ's blood. An *Annunciation* might be expected on the outside of the wings, but the original could have been a fixed or folding triptych.

Whatever the subjects of the missing paintings, two more being the minimum required for symmetry, the size of the *Crucifixion* would make it the central picture of the altarpiece. The *Resurrection*, last in any narrative sequence, should logically occupy the lower right, with the preceding event of the *Entombment* above. Narrative cannot be relied on to proceed logically in fifteenth-century art but the design of the two pictures strongly supports this ordering.

The two compositions are emphatically open to the left and closed to the right, with the tomb cut by the left edge but contained by the right. The focus of interest in the *Entombment*, Christ's head and torso, is well to the left and the narrowed back of Nicodemus (?) sharply closes the frieze of figures to the right, as does the soldier in the *Resurrection*, whose falling scarf contrives his straight outline. On the left side, the vertical of the angel is softened by his swirling cloak. Both pictures urge the viewer to imitate the painted figures and look to the left, where the rest of the altarpiece would be.

Similarly, the angular verticals of the *Entombment* lead the eye downwards, where attention would be caught in the *Resurrection* by the angel, Christ's banner and the three Maries, elements which animate the picture surface to a higher level than that of the *Entombment*, with its unrelieved sky and landscapes. The curving draperies of the resurrected Christ and the angel redirect attention upwards, while the sleeping soldier is an effective concluding form below. The counterpointing of horizontal and vertical within and between these paintings reinforces the meaning of each by the reversed patterning running through them as a pair. Christ's slumped body, for example, supported by upright figures, changes to the standing Christ surrounded by seated or prone figures. In colour too, the *Entombment*, although more worn, seems intended to convey a pale evening light, which shifts in the *Resurrection* to the dawn, where red predominates. The avoidance of monotony is surely the only reason for the altered landscape, whereas the altered light is not only required by the narrative but becomes a major factor in the expressive content of the pictures.

The *Entombment* is usually dated early in Bouts's career. Comparatively crude in landscape construction and clumsy in some of the figure drawing, both *Entombment* and *Resurrection* are derived from Rogier van der Weyden's *Miraflores Triptych*. The *Crucifixion*, with mounted soldiers, fits more into northern Netherlandish traditions, a combination of sources which accords with Bouts's earlier years when he first moved south to Louvain and was exposed to van der Weyden's art. There is no evidence beyond Eastlake's mention of the Foscari to say for whom these pictures were made. Francesco Foscari, Doge from 1423 to 1457, consolidated the fortunes of this Venetian family but little appears to be known about their patronage of art. Commission for export might explain the unusual cloth support. If this altarpiece were in Venice in the mid fifteenth century, its surviving pictures may prove of great importance, not only for the history of Netherlandish painting but also for understanding the development of Venetian art.

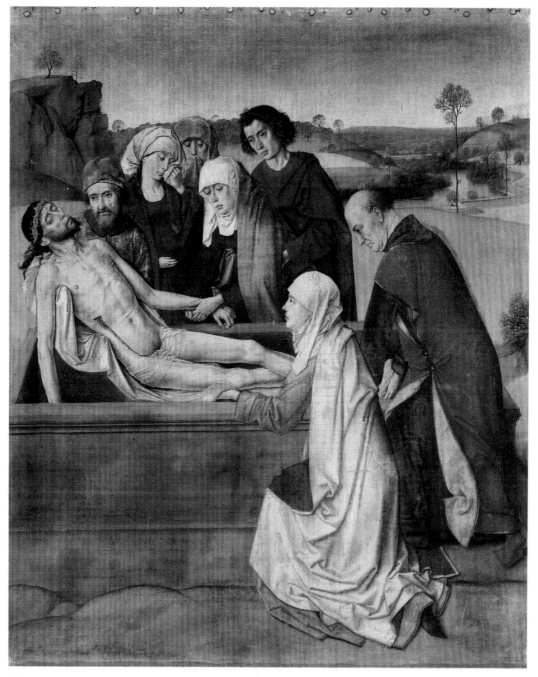

Fig 2
DIERIC BOUTS
The Entombment
Tempera on cotton, mid fifteenth century, 35$\frac{3}{8}$in by 29$\frac{1}{4}$in (90cm by 74.5cm)
In the National Gallery, London

FRANCESCO GUARDI
The portico and courtyard of a Venetian palace
On copper, 5in by 7in (12.5cm by 18cm)
London £50,000 ($117,500). 12.XII.79

LUCA CARLEVARIS
Venice: the piazzetta seen from the north
48in by 63½in (122cm by 161.5cm)
London £40,000 ($94,000). 16.VII.80

GIOVANNI BATTISTA TIEPOLO
The Last Judgement
57½in by 78¾in (146cm by 200cm)
Florence L260,000,000 (£132,383:$311,100). 6.V.80

HUBERT ROBERT
An Egyptian fantasy
Signed and dated *Roma 1760*, 25in by 37½in (63.5cm by 95.5cm)
New York $85,000 (£36,170). 9.I.80

JOSEPH VERNET
A Mediterranean port at sunset
Signed and dated *Roma 1751*, 26⅜in by 33⅞in (67cm by 86cm)
Monte Carlo FF610,000 (£62,887:$147,784). 26.V.80

SALOMON VAN RUYSDAEL
A river landscape with peasants ferrying cattle
On panel, signed and dated *1633*, 14½in by 20in (37cm by 51cm)
London £42,000 ($98,700). 16.VII.80

JACOB MARREL
A still life
On copper, signed, 7$\frac{1}{4}$in by 5$\frac{1}{2}$in (18.5cm by 14cm)
London £51,000 ($119,850). 12.XII.79

JANUARIUS ZICK
An evening scene with peasants outside an inn
One of a pair, signed, 21¾in by 15½in (55cm by 39.5cm)
London £28,000 ($65,800). 16.VII.80

DAVID TENIERS THE YOUNGER
Villagers outside an inn
Signed and dated *1654*, 22in by 33in (56cm by 84cm)
New York $230,000 (£97,872). 9.I.80

NICOLAES BERCHEM
A winter scene
Signed and dated *1652,* 26in by 32in (66cm by 81.5cm)
London £100,000 ($235,000). 16.IV.80

PIETER BRUEGHEL THE YOUNGER
The return from a village fair
On panel, signed, 17¾in by 24in (45cm by 61cm)
London £170,000 ($399,500). 12.XII.79

PIETER JANSZ. SAENREDAM
Interior of the church of St Cunera at Rhenen
On panel, 19¼in by 27¼in (49cm by 69cm)
London £52,000 ($122,200). 16.IV.80

HANS BOL
An extensive landscape with Elisha and the children of Beth-el in the foreground
Gouache heightened with gold on vellum, 5⅜in by 7⅞in (13.8cm by 20.1cm)
Amsterdam Fl 110,000 (£24,176 : $56,813). 29.X.79

JAN BRUEGHEL THE YOUNGER
Travellers and wagons on a road, a town in the distance
Gouache on vellum, 7¾in by 9⅛in (18.8cm by 23.2cm)
Amsterdam Fl 104,000 (£22,857 : $53,714). 29.X.79

JACOB DE GHEYN II
Study of a tree
Pen and brown ink, 13¾in by 7¾in
(35cm by 19.8cm)
London £6,200 ($14,570). 10.XII.79

SIR PETER PAUL RUBENS
Studies of figures for The fall of the Damned
Black and white chalk on grey paper, *circa* 1621,
12⅝in by 10⅜in (32cm by 26.3cm)
Amsterdam Fl 115,000 (£25,275 : $59,396). 29.X.79

JAN VAN GOYEN
A market scene with a charlatan addressing a crowd
Black chalk and grey wash, signed and dated *1656*, 6¾in by 10½in
(17.2cm by 26.8cm)
Amsterdam Fl 74,000 (£16,264 : $38,220). 29.X.79

BALDASSARE FRANCESCHINI called IL VOLTERRANO
Study for The Rest on the Flight into Egypt
Black chalk, 11½in by 8⅜in (29.2cm by 21.4cm)
London £3,700 ($8,695). 3.VII.80

This drawing comes from a collection of almost
200 previously unpublished drawings
by Volterrano

PIER LEONE GHEZZI
*Cardinal Polignac, Father Agliata, The Abbot of
St Germain, Abbé Le Blond, and Ghezzi*
Pen and brown ink, *circa* 1725, from a group of
152 drawings by Ghezzi, 12½in by 12⅝in
(31.7cm by 32.2cm)
London £1,700 ($3,995). 10.XII.79
From the collection of the Rt Hon.
Lord Braybrooke

GIOVANNI DOMENICO TIEPOLO
Punchinello's mistress faints
Pen, brown ink and wash over
black chalk, signed, *circa* 1800,
14⅛in by 18¾in (35.8cm by 47.5cm)
London £27,000 ($63,450). 3.VII.80

HUBERT ROBERT
Vue d'une cour, villa Pamphili
Pen, brown and black ink and wash, signed and dated *A ROMAE 1762,*
12⅝in by 17⅝in (32cm by 44.9cm)
Monte Carlo FF140,000 (£14,433: $33,918). 26.XI.79
From the collection of Claude Cartier

GIOVANNI BATTISTA PIRANESI
An architectural study in reverse for a print in Opere varie, 1750
Pen, brown ink and grey wash, signed, 5⅜in by 7¾in (13.7cm by 19.8cm)
London £22,000 ($51,700). 3.VII.80

JEAN–ETIENNE LIOTARD
Portrait of a woman in Maltese costume
Pastel, *circa* 1738, 32½in by 21⅛in (82.5cm by 53.5cm)
London £68,000 ($159,800). 10.XII.79

JACQUES-ANDRE PORTAIL
Femme assise, vue à mi-corps
Red and black chalk, signed, $11\frac{3}{4}$in by $8\frac{1}{4}$in (29.9cm by 21cm)
Monte Carlo FF145,000 (£14,948 : $35,129). 26.XI.79
From the collection of Claude Cartier

THOMAS GIRTIN
Bamborough Castle, Northumberland
Watercolour and pencil, signed and dated *1797*, inscribed with the title on the reverse, 16½in by 21½in
(42cm by 54.5cm)
London £25,000 ($58,750). 13.III.80
From the collection of the late Sir Geoffrey Selby Church

EDWARD LEAR
Water shrews
Watercolour and pencil, signed and dated *August 14th 1832*, inscribed with the title on the reverse,
4½in by 9½in (11.5cm by 24cm)
London £3,000 ($7,050). 13.III.80
From the collection of Miss M. Norton

JOSEPH MALLORD WILLIAM TURNER, RA
Sidon
Watercolour, *circa* 1833, 5$\frac{1}{4}$in by 8$\frac{1}{8}$in (13.5cm by 20.5cm)
London £31,000 ($72,850). 13.III.80
From the collection of the late Mrs E. M. Harvey-Samuel

This watercolour is based on a drawing by Charles Barry, and is one of the series engraved by William and Edward Finden for their *Landscape Illustrations of the Bible* (1835–36)

Opposite
RICHARD PARKES BONINGTON
Fishing boats with fishermen mending nets on the shore – an estuary beyond
Watercolour, signed, *circa* 1823, 7in by 9$\frac{1}{4}$in (18cm by 23.5cm)
London £13,000 ($30,550). 13.III.80

JOHN FREDERICK LEWIS, RA
The mid-day meal, Cairo
Watercolour and bodycolour with gum arabic, signed and dated *1875*, 19½in by 25in
(49.5cm by 63.5cm)
London £75,000 ($176,250). 22.XI.79
From the collection of Mrs E. Gallop

JOSHUA CRISTALL
Girl going to market, Binstead, Isle of Wight
Watercolour with gum arabic and pencil, signed, numbered *4* and dated *1815*, 17in by 13¼in
(43cm by 33.5cm)
London £3,600 ($8,460). 10.VII.80

JOHN CONSTABLE, RA
Flatford Lock
Circa 1810, 7¾in by 12¾in (19.5cm by 32.5cm)
New York $155,000 (£65,957). 29.V.80

RICHARD PARKES BONINGTON
A view of Lerici
On board, 1826, 14in by 18in (35.5cm by 45.5cm)
London £65,000 ($152,750). 12.III.80

JOSEPH MALLORD WILLIAM TURNER, RA
Juliet and her nurse
Circa 1836, 36¼in by 48½in (92cm by 123cm)
New York $6,400,000 (£2,723,404). 29.V.80
From the collection of Flora Whitney Miller

A splendid deception:
Turner's *Juliet and her nurse*

Martin Butlin

Juliet and her nurse (see opposite), exhibited by J. M. W. Turner at the Royal Academy in 1836, is perhaps the most splendid of all Turner's paintings of the 1830s. But, together with *Mercury and Argus* and to a lesser extent *Rome, from Mount Aventine*, the other works exhibited in 1836, it was the occasion for one of the most vituperative attacks on Turner's later style. This was from the Rev. John Eagles, writing in *Blackwood's Magazine*. Eagles, a failed artist, who had modelled his style on Gaspard Poussin and Salvator Rosa, not unnaturally found Turner's later style difficult to understand, but his criticism went far beyond mere disapproval.

This is indeed a strange jumble – 'confusion worse confounded'. It is neither sunlight, moonlight, nor starlight, nor firelight, though there is an attempt at a display of fireworks in one corner, and we conjecture that these are meant to be stars in the heavens – if so, it is a verification of Hamlet's extravagant madness –

'Doubt that the stars are fire;
Doubt that the sun doth move;
Doubt Truth to be a liar;'

but with such a Juliet you would certainly doubt 'I love'. Amidst so many absurdities, we scarcely stop to ask why Juliet and her nurse should be at Venice. For the scene is a composition as from models of different parts of Venice, thrown higgledy-piggledy together, streaked blue and pink, and thrown into a flour tub. Poor Juliet has been steeped in treacle to make her look sweet, and we feel apprehensive lest the mealy architecture should stick to her petticoat, and flour it.

Not all the critics were unfavourable (indeed the *Morning Herald* described it as 'a vision of night; it is quite dreamy and poetic, and the tone of colour harmonises with the scene'), but *The Times* was nearly as abusive, asking why Turner could not confine himself to 'poetical landscape, instead of aspiring to represent Shakespeare's Juliet? Shakespeare's Juliet? Why, it is the tawdry Miss Porringer, the brazier's daughter of Lambeth Marsh, and the nurse is the twaddling old body Mrs Mac'sneeze, who keeps the snuff-shop at the corner of Oakley-street'.

It was the Rev. John Eagles's review in *Blackwood's Magazine* that provoked the young John Ruskin into his defence of Turner, a defence that eventually turned into the five volumes of *Modern Painters*. In its original form, a mere 2,000 words, Ruskin intended it as a reply to be published in *Blackwood's Magazine* itself, but on his father's advice, he sent his draft to Turner who dissuaded him: after thanking Ruskin for 'your zeal, kindness, and the trouble you have taken in my behalf', Turner went on, 'I never move in these matters. They are of no import save mischief and the meal tub'; he ended by asking if he could send the manuscript on to H. A. J. Munro of Novar, who had bought the picture at the Royal Academy.

Ruskin begins by pointing out that Turner's view of Venice, far from being 'higgledy-piggledy', is accurate in every particular. He explains that, as an imaginative artist, Turner does not paint nature but rather from nature, and extols his technique: 'he can produce instantaneous effect by a roll of his brush, and, with a few dashes of mingled colour, will express the most complicated subject: the means employed appear more astonishingly inadequate for the effect produced than in any other master'. He continues, attacking Eagles's criticisms one by one, and sums up by claiming that Turner's 'imagination is Shakespearian in its mightiness'.

Ruskin says nothing of Turner's having placed Juliet and her nurse in Venice rather than Verona, though this was a point taken up by a number of other critics besides Eagles. One might be content, with the critic of the *Spectator*, to shrug one's shoulders over Turner's title – 'it might as well have been called anything else' – were it not for the fact that a leading American Turner expert has suggested that Turner was not referring to Shakespeare at all but to Samuel Rogers's account in *Italy*, published in 1830, of how the 'Lovely Giulietta' mourned her unjustly executed fiancé Marcolini, losing her reason: 'every night, when the great square of San Marco is illuminating and the casinos are filling fast with the gay and the dissipated, a bell is rung as for a service, and a ray of light seen to issue from the small gothic window that looks towards the place of execution, the place where on a scaffold MARCOLINI breathed his last'. The square form on the left-hand side of the piazza is seen by this critic as the scaffold.

However, Turner would have had to have been more than usually perverse to have been alluding to Rogers rather than to Shakespeare. Not only did he fail to respond to any of the criticisms of his choice of subject (it would not have been out of character for Turner, with a certain sardonic delight, to leave his critics in ignorance), but he did not even bother to inform Ruskin that he had made a mistake, if a mistake it was. Turner included no quotation or reference in the Royal Academy catalogue, though this was frequently his practice. He must surely, therefore, have assumed that his public would make, unaided, the most obvious identification of the subject, Shakespeare's 'Juliet' rather than Rogers's 'Giulietta', the Italian version of the name used by Rogers throughout. There is no nurse in Rogers's account, nor in the picture is there a gothic window from which a ray of light can be 'seen to issue'. When looking at the picture itself it is difficult to accept that the so-called scaffold on the left is the main centre or even one of the main centres of the composition. If anything is the main centre, it is the glow of light in the middle of the painting, with a subsidiary focus on the right where the bursting rockets emphasise the two figures standing on the balcony below. Moreover, though Turner's paintings, and even his Venetian subjects such as *The sun of Venice going to sea*, often embody Turner's habitual pessimism, despite their radiant and seemingly positive appearance, it is difficult when looking at *Juliet and her nurse* to find any real echo of Rogers's morbid subject, when the scene would have to show the tragic aftermath of the execution of the girl's lover. It is much easier to see it as a festive scene, albeit one concealing within the glamour and excitement evoked by the Capulets' party, the seeds of the tragedy that is to come.

Further light, if not total clarification, is cast by Hollis's engraving of the picture, published in 1842 by Turner's dealer Thomas Griffiths 'for J. M. W. Turner, R.A.', and with the name of H. A. J. Munro of Novar, who had bought the original oil painting at the Royal Academy in 1836, 'To whom this Engraving is most respectfully dedicated by J.M.W. Turner'. The engraving was thus clearly issued with Turner's blessing, but under what title? 'S͎ MARK'S PLACE, VENICE. (*Moonlight*)'. Now at last Turner even adds verses to clarify the subject, or so one would think, but what he quotes are four lines from Byron's *Childe Harold's Pilgrimage*, slightly condensed in form, alluding to Venice's former glories:

> . . . but Beauty doth not die –
> Nor yet forget how Venice once was dear –
> The pleasant place of all festivity
> The revels of the earth, the Masque of Italy.

The form on the left of the piazza, the precise nature of which cannot be seen in the painting, is quite clearly in the engraving a Punch and Judy show. This is, incidentally, one of the least well-attended entertainments in the piazza. The great glow of light on the other side of the square now contains a clearly depicted cross. The inference is, surely, that Turner, stung by the criticisms when he first exhibited his painting, has made his subject less specific. The theme of the passing of a town's or country's former glory was one which he frequently expressed, and he had exhibited pictures with quotations from *Childe Harold's Pilgrimage* on previous occasions.

There is a broader lesson to be learned from Turner's apparent casualness over subject matter. He was not as interested in specific subjects as he was in the general mood of his pictures. What better place for a story of 'star-cross'd' young lovers than Venice by night? Twentieth-century ingeniousness seems no substitute for the understanding approach of the critic of the *Morning Post* for 25 May 1836.

No. 73 'Juliet and her Nurse'. This is one of those magical pictures by which Mr. Turner dazzles the sense and storms the imagination. Vague, indistinct, with a lavish display of colour, unequalled and unapproachable, this picture is a perfect scene of enchantment. It might be called a carnival, or any other name that a festive crowd might suggest. Vessels in the distance, rockets cleaving the sky, gay attire, and everything that can combine to complete the gorgeous are here, and so we suppose are Juliet and the nurse in the balcony, for there is an indication of a balcony and female forms. But the merit of the picture is in its appeal through the medium of colour to the imagination, and a more astonishing appeal was never made nor a more splendid deception ever witnessed.

HENRY BERNARD CHALON
Sir Mark Masterman Sykes' hounds
Signed and dated *1820*, 34½in by 47in (87.5cm by 119.5cm)
London £50,000 ($117,500). 9.VII.80
From the collection of Viscountess Monckton of Brenchley

HENRY BERNARD CHALON
Portrait of the Bower family with their hunters
Signed and dated 1824. 51¼in by 66¾in (130cm by 169.5cm)
London £36,000 ($84,600). 9.VII.80
From the collection of Viscountess Monckton of Brenchley

JOHANN BAPTIST CLOSTERMAN
Portrait of the children of John Taylor of Bifrons
Circa 1702, 74½in by 107in (189cm by 272cm)
London £15,000 ($35,250). 9.VII.80
From the collection of the late Brian Morley Crosbie Trench

JOHANN HEINRICH FUSELI, RA
Lapland orgies
Circa 1794, 39½in by 49½in (100.5cm by 126cm)
London £22,000 ($51,700). 9.VII.80

This painting illustrates a passage from Book II of Milton's *Paradise Lost* and was executed as one of a series for the Milton Gallery, which opened in London in 1799 as a rival undertaking to Boydell's Shakespeare Gallery

JOHN SINGLETON COPLEY, RA
Portrait of George Boone Roupell
Circa 1779, 78in by 52in (198cm by 132cm)
London £110,000 ($258,500). 21.XI.79
From the collection of Lt-Col. P. G. Roupell

GEORGE STUBBS, ARA
Portrait of Joseph Smyth, Esq., mounted on a grey hunter, an extensive river landscape beyond
Early 1760s, 24½in by 29½in (62cm by 75cm)
London £100,000 ($235,000). 9.VII.80

HENRY STACY MARKS, RA
The ornithologist
Signed and dated *1873*, signed on the reverse, 52in by 38½in (132cm by 98cm)
New York $34,000 (£14,468). 29.V.80

This painting was exhibited at the Royal Academy in 1873

JOHN FREDERICK HERRING SR
Shoeing a white horse
Signed and dated *1856*, 33½in by 43¼in (85cm by 110cm)
Belgravia £31,500 ($74,025). 1.X.79

SIR LAWRENCE ALMA-TADEMA, OM, RA
Caracalla and Geta, bear fight in the Coliseum 203 AD
Signed and numbered *Op.CCCLXXXII*, in a frame designed by the artist, 1905–1907, 48½in by 60½in
(123cm by 153.5cm)
Belgravia £145,000($340,750). 9.IV.80

CHARLES GREEN
Her first bouquet: the Lane family with Lupino at the Britannia Theatre, Hoxton
Watercolour, signed and dated *1869*, 21½in by 31in (54.5cm by 79cm)
Belgravia £12,500 ($29,375). 1.X.79

SIR EDWARD COLEY BURNE-JONES, ARA
The sleep of King Arthur in Avalon
Gouache, signed, inscribed *to E.L.* and dated *1894*, 23½in by 77½in (59.5cm by 197cm)
Belgravia £30,000 ($70,500). 1.X.79

SIR EDWARD COLEY BURNE-JONES, ARA
The star of Bethlehem
Gouache and gold paint, *circa* 1885, 24½in by 39in (62cm by 99cm)
Belgravia £30,000 ($70,500). 1.X.79

SIR EDWARD COLEY BURNE-JONES, ARA
The heart of the rose
Signed and dated *1889*, 38in by 51½in (96.5cm by 131cm)
Belgravia £130,000 ($305,500). 9.IV.80

The Romance of the Rose, a verse by William Morris after Chaucer, was written especially for this painting and is inscribed on the frame

> The ending of the tale ye see;
> The Lover draws anigh the tree,
> And takes the branch, and takes the rose,
> That love and he so dearly chose.

ALBERT JOSEPH MOORE, ARWS
A garden
Signed with anthemion device and dated *1869*,
68in by 33½in (172.5cm by 85cm)
Belgravia £22,000 ($51,700). 1.X.79

This painting was exhibited at the Royal Academy in 1870,
and is now in the Tate Gallery

JACQUES JOSEPH TISSOT
Le veuf
On panel, signed, *circa* 1876, 14in by 9¼in (35.5cm by 23.5cm)
Belgravia £24,000 ($56,400). 1.X.79

CHARLES SIMS, RA, RWS
Butterflies
Signed, 47½in by 53½in (120.5cm by 136cm)
Belgravia £15,500 ($36,425). 9.IV.80

This painting was exhibited at the Royal Academy in 1904

CHARLES ALLSTON COLLINS
May in the Regent's Park
On panel, signed and dated *1851*, inscribed with the title on a label on the reverse, $17\frac{1}{2}$in by $27\frac{1}{2}$in
(44.5cm by 70cm)
Belgravia £16,000 ($37,600). 1.X.79

This painting was exhibited at the Royal Academy in 1852, and is now in the Tate Gallery

AUGUSTUS JOHN, OM, RA
Portrait of Trelawnay Dayrell Reed
Signed, 1918, 24⅛in by 16⅛in (61.5cm by 41cm)
London £19,000 ($44,650). 25.VI.80

SPENCER GORE
The Mad Pierrot ballet at the Alhambra
Signed, *circa* 1905, 17in by 21¼in (43cm by 54cm)
London £9,000 ($21,150). 25.VI.80

HAROLD KNIGHT, RA
A village wedding
Circa 1908, 63½in by 75¼in
(161.5cm by 191cm)
London £9,800 ($23,030). 5.III.80
From the collection of Jane
Alexander

Fig 1
WALTER RICHARD SICKERT, ARA
The Camden Town murder ('What shall we do about the rent?')
Signed, *circa* 1908, 9⅝in by 13½in (24.5cm by 34.5cm)
London £23,500 ($55,225). 14.XI.79

Sickert and the Camden Town Murder

Wendy Baron

On 12 September 1907 Emily Dimmock, an attractive, tall, blonde, twenty-two-year-old prostitute well-known in the pubs and music halls of north London, was found in her lodgings at 29 St Paul's Road, Camden Town, with her throat cut. She had been murdered in the early hours of the morning as she slept. Her naked body was discovered by Bertram Shaw, the man with whom she lived, when he returned from his night-shift duty as a cook on the London to Sheffield run of a Midland railway restaurant car. She was lying face downwards on her left side, her hair in curling pins, her left arm tucked behind her, and her right resting on the pillow.

The Camden Town Murder, as it was immediately christened by the press, was prominently reported in popular and serious newspapers over the next three months. While the inquest was in progress Robert Wood, a commercial artist, was arrested. The police court hearing was followed by a trial during which a vivid portrait of Camden Town low-life emerged as a succession of witnesses provided information about Miss Dimmock's recent past and her associates. The evidence against Wood was circumstantial and contradictory; a week before Christmas he was discharged as not guilty. The case remained unsolved.

Sickert spent the summer of 1907 in London, so engrossed in a series of interiors painted in his rooms at 6 Mornington Crescent that he delayed his usual July departure for France by up to two months. He had probably arrived in Dieppe 'to do landscapes for the weaker brethren' by the date of the murder, but he might well have reflected on reading press reports that he had spent every alternate day in recent months in a Camden Town bedsitter, painting a nude model who perhaps supplemented her earnings by following Miss Dimmock's trade.

For the first twenty years of his career Sickert had painted music halls, landscapes and portraits. He was forty-two years old when he began to develop his interest in the intimate figure subjects with which his name is instantly associated. In 1902 he drew his mistress, the handsome doyenne of the Dieppe fishmarket, nude on a bed. Then, during the winter of 1903–1904, in his rooms in Venice, he painted studies of the local prostitutes, usually clothed and sometimes together in two-figure groups. When he returned to live in London in 1905, after seven years abroad, Sickert continued to explore such subjects, gradually integrating his figures and their settings into ever more convincing interior compositions. Around Easter 1906 the Belgian Daurmont sisters posed together, decorously clothed as suited their respectable status, in his Fitzroy Street studio. Meanwhile, his presentation of nude models on iron bedsteads gained authority as he added accessory details to establish the bedroom ambience more fully. The Mornington Crescent nudes of 1907 represent the climax of this effort. Among the most accomplished of these paintings is a tenderly handled back-view of a nude seated on the far side of a bed. This was the springboard for perhaps the first of Sickert's compositions to be called *The Camden Town murder*.

The relationships of Sickert's drawings to his paintings and to each other are seldom straightforward. An idea in one study would inspire another until he had produced a consequential series of variations capable of development in many directions. At some stage in 1908 Sickert alighted on a drawing of a back-view seated nude related to the Mornington Crescent painting and, by adding the figure of a clothed man seated beside her, radically altered the psychological meaning of the work. He produced an etching of this composition and called it *The Camden Town murder*. Again in 1908, using the same male model, Sickert both drew and etched another composition of a nude woman and clothed man on a bed, apparently about to embrace, entitled, alternatively, *La belle gatée* or *The Camden Town murder*. The models and the bed represented in *La belle gatée*, all re-deployed compositionally, appear in Sickert's earliest painting to be given the *Camden Town murder* title (Fig 1). This little painting, so dense and powerful that it is hard to credit its true dimensions from an illustration, was Sickert's first essay in oils on the clothed man/naked woman theme.

Neither the prints nor the painting were illustrations of the murder. Indeed, the painting is also known as '*What shall we do about the rent?*', the title Sickert inscribed some twenty years later on sketches for the picture still in his studio. However, the *Murder* title was not just drawn out of a hat for publicity purposes. The event itself fired Sickert's imagination. It drew his attention as an artist to the real-life tragedies daily enacted around him in the back streets of Camden Town, to the struggle for survival among the poor and deprived, for whom the sale of a woman's body was one of the few available options. Thus, the question posed in the title '*What shall we do about the rent?*' is not necessarily inconsistent with a subject purporting to illustrate an episode in the life-history of a prostitute.

There is an oral tradition, on the whole supported by drawn impressions of the accused published in the *News of the World*, that Sickert employed Robert Wood as his model. Certainly, the man represented in the prints and painting described above reappears, together with a nude, in five more paintings of 1908 and 1909. Two of these paintings, *Home life* and *Dawn, Camden Town* (the latter originally entitled *Summer in Naples*) have never been named *The Camden Town murder*. Two more closely interrelated paintings, each showing the man seated on a bed looking down towards a nude stretched alongside, were exhibited in London in 1911, and perhaps in Paris in 1909, under the *Murder* title. However, both have also been called '*What shall we do about the rent?*', and one of the versions has a third title, *Summer afternoon*. The fifth painting, *L'affaire de Camden Town* (Fig 2), bought by Paul Signac at a sale of Sickert's work in Paris in 1909, has never had an alternative title. It is the most brutal in design, mood and handling, and thus by far the most convincing as an illustration of the murder. Moreover, Sickert confirmed the explicit relationship of the picture and its ostensible subject when, in the later 1920s, he inscribed a drawing of the twisted figure of the nude, *Study for murder of Emily Dimmock in St. Paul's Road*

Fig 2
WALTER RICHARD SICKERT, ARA
L'affaire de Camden Town
Signed, *circa* 1908, 23½in by 15½in
(59.5cm by 39.5cm)
London £14,000. 14.III.73

Camden Town. Nevertheless, even this painting does not present an episode of the actual murder. Sickert developed his image of threatening violence from a delicate drawing of two women in intimate conversation. He did not build his design upon a basis of known facts. The woman in his painting is dark-haired and wears no curling pins. Emily Dimmock was killed unawares as she slept, face downwards, but Sickert has shown a moment of confrontation between the supine, naked woman and the clothed man towering above.

The *Camden Town murder* title must be recognised as generic rather than specific, although we may accept that the murder itself first inspired Sickert to juxtapose a clothed man and a naked woman in his figure subjects. This juxtaposition profoundly shocked his public, just as Manet's modern dress transformation of Giorgione's rustic idyll, *Le déjeuner sur l'herbe*, had shocked the French in 1863. Sickert, however, used no art historical reference to soften the impact of his paintings. He boldly presented the figures as protagonists in intimate, even sordid, dramas of contemporary lower-class life. Whether or not titular acknowledgement was made to the notorious murder, his two-figure man and woman paintings have a realistic, documentary character unprecedented in British art. Although his paintings were not illustrations of real-life events, they read as if they were. Indeed, literature, rather than the visual arts, perhaps influenced his treatment of these themes. As Sickert was to write in 1912: 'All the greater draughtsmen tell a story'. After years of observing, memorising and recording, Sickert used the accumulated wealth of his documentary material, like a novelist of the Realist school, to construct compelling works of fiction.

SIR ALFRED MUNNINGS, PRA
The start at Newmarket
On board, signed, 36¼in by 72in (92cm by 183cm)
London £126,000 ($296,100). 25.VI.80
From the collection of D. E. Cotton

MONTAGUE DAWSON
Summer morning
Signed, 24in by 36in (61cm by 91.5cm)
New York $47,500 (£20,213). 29.V.80
From the collection of Donald J. Clifford

WALTER LANGLEY
The greeting
Signed and dated *1904*, 48in by 60in (122cm by 152.5cm)
London £11,500 ($27,025). 25.VI.80

JOHN PETER RUSSELL
Belle Ile
Signed, inscribed *Au Docteur
Forest de Faye* and dated *1905*,
26in by 32in (66cm by 81.5cm)
London £11,500 ($27,025).
25.VI.80

EDWARD SEAGO
Highmill Farm, Norfolk
On board, signed, 22in by 36in (56cm by 91.5cm)
London £12,500 ($29,375). 5.III.80

ROMAN SCHOOL, NINETEENTH CENTURY
Project for a large silver terrine
Pen, Indian ink and grey wash, *circa* 1805–
1815, 23½in by 24¼in (59.5cm by 61.5cm)
London £3,000 ($7,050). 19.VI.80

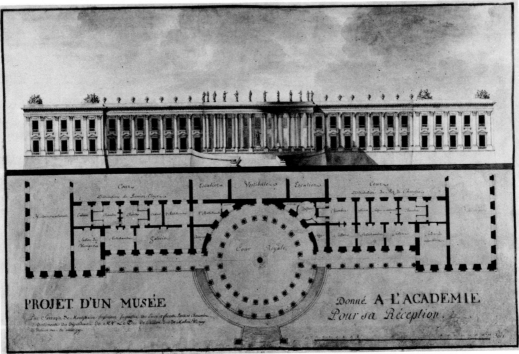

SARRAZIN DE MONTFERRIER
Projet d'un musée – donné à l'Académie pour sa réception
Pen, Indian ink and watercolour, inscribed and dated *aoust 1787*, 20¾in by 32in (52.5cm by 81.5cm)
London £4,300 ($10,105). 19.VI.80

LOUIS-LEOPOLD BOILLY
La paresseuse
Black and white chalk heightened with white gouache on buff paper, signed, *circa* 1790, 19½in by
15⅝in (49.5cm by 39.5cm)
New York $35,000 (£14,894). 3.VI.80
From the collection of the late Clarence Dillon

LOUIS-LEOPOLD BOILLY
La descente de diligence
Circa 1803, 16⅛in by 13⅜in (41cm by 34cm)
Monte Carlo FF490,000 (£50,515:$118,711). 26.XI.79
From the collection of Claude Cartier

CARL GEORG ADOLPHE HASENPFLUG
Potsdam – die Garnisonkirche
On copper, signed and dated *1827*, 25½in by 33in (65cm by 84cm)
London £27,000 ($63,450). 19.III.80

CORNELIS SPRINGER
A market square, Zierikzee, Zeeland
Signed and dated 1858, 18¼in by 23in (46.5cm by 58.5cm)
New York $70,000 (£29,787). 25.I.80
From the collection of Pamela McAneny

BAREND CORNELIS KOEKKOEK
Drovers on a country lane by the Rhine
On panel, signed and dated 1854, signed and stamped with the artist's seal on a label on the reverse,
20¾in by 29in (52.5cm by 73.5cm)
London £70,000 ($164,500). 19.III.80
From the collection of the Hon. Mrs Pretyman

FRIEDRICH GAUERMAN
After the hunt
On panel, signed and dated *1857*, $33\frac{1}{2}$in by $41\frac{1}{2}$in (85cm by 105.5cm)
New York $60,000 (£25,532). 29.V.80

JOHANN GEORG MEYER VON BREMEN
Auf dem Heimwege
Signed and dated *Berlin 1883*, 34in by 44½in (86.5cm by 113cm)
New York $100,000 (£42,553). 25.I.80
From the collection of Mr and Mrs Eugene Ferkauf

EUGENE DELACROIX
Cheval effrayé par l'orage
Watercolour and gouache on buff paper, signed, *circa* 1824–27, $5\frac{1}{4}$in by 7in (13.5cm by 18cm)
New York $42,000 (£17,872). 12.X.79

KARL PAVLOVICH BRIULLOV
Portrait of P.A. Chikhachev, the geologist and geographer
Watercolour and pencil, signed and inscribed, *circa* 1835, $13\frac{1}{4}$in by $16\frac{3}{4}$in (33.5cm by 42.5cm)
London £10,000 ($23,500). 13.V.80

LUIGI LOIR
Visitors at the 1878 Paris 'Exposition Universelle'
Gouache, pencil, pen and ink, signed and dated 78,
13in by 18½in (33cm by 47cm)
London £6,800 ($15,980). 19.VI.80

GIUSEPPE DE NITTIS
Ritratto della moglie
12⅝in by 9¼in (32cm by 23.5cm)
Florence L 22,000,000 (£11,202:$26,324). 6.V.80

JEAN BERAUD
Le bal public
Signed and dated *1880*, 30½in by 48⅞in (77.5cm by 124cm)
Los Angeles $150,000 (£63,830). 23.VI.80
From the collection of the late Charles Boyer

PIERRE PUVIS DE CHAVANNES
Le repos
Signed, inscribed *à son ami Claude* and dated *61*, 24¼in by 35in (61.5cm by 89cm)
London £32,000 ($75,200). 28.XI.79

This is a study for one of the four earliest paintings in the group known as *Le cycle d'Amiens*

JEAN-FRANCOIS MILLET
Le cheval du paysan
Pastel, signed, *circa* 1869, 26¾in by 36¾in (67.5cm by 93.5cm)
London £49,000($115,150). 19.VI.80

JEAN LEON GEROME
Le maître d'équipage nègre
Signed, *circa* 1876, 13in by 9¾in (33cm by 25cm)
New York $52,500 (£22,340). 29.V.80

JOAQUIN SOROLLA Y BASTIDA
Pescadores valencianas
Signed and dated 1903, 36¼in by 49¾in (93cm by 126.5cm)
London £140,000 ($329,000). 28.XI.79

GIUSEPPE PELLIZZA DA VOLPEDO
Mammine
Signed and dated *1892*, 85¾in by 80in (218cm by 203cm)
London £70,000($164,500). 18.VI.80

GIUSEPPE PELLIZZA DA VOLPEDO
Idillio primaverile
Signed three times and twice dated *1901*, signed and dated *1896–1901* on the reverse,
diameter 39¼in (99.5cm)
London £165,000 ($387,750). 18.VI.80
From the collection of A. A. N. Carswell

EDGAR DEGAS
Deux danseuses au repos
Pastel on green paper, signed, 19in by 25in (48cm by 63.5cm)
New York $180,000 (£76,596). 7.XI.79
From the collection of Paulette Goddard Remarque

PIERRE-AUGUSTE RENOIR
Les baigneuses
Pastel, signed, 1894, 18¾in by 15¾in (47.5cm by 40cm)
London £190,000 ($446,500). 1.VII.80

CAMILLE PISSARRO
Paysage aux environs de Louveciennes (automne)
Signed and dated 1870, 35½in by 45¾in (90cm by 116cm)
London £165,000($387,750). 5.XII.79
From the collection of Roger Goldet

ALFRED SISLEY
La Seine à Bougival
Signed and dated '73, 13½in by 18½in (34.5cm by 47cm)
London £125,000($293,750). 26.III.80

CLAUDE MONET
Vase de pivoines
Signed, 1882, 39½in by 32in (100.5cm by 81.5cm)
London £280,000 ($658,000). 26.III.80

JAMES ENSOR
Squelettes à l'atelier
Signed and dated *1900*, 43¾in by 31¼in (111cm by 79.5cm)
London £110,000 ($258,500). 26.III.80
From the collection of Suzanne Janson-Hallet

VINCENT VAN GOGH
Portrait d'Adeline Ravoux
1890, 28½in by 21in (72.5cm by 53.5cm)
New York $1,800,000 (£765,957). 12.V.80
From the collection of the late Edgar William and Bernice Chrysler Garbisch

Adeline Ravoux was the sixteen-year-old daughter of the artist's host in Auvers in the
summer of 1890

HENRI DE TOULOUSE-LAUTREC
Femme assise dans un jardin
On panel, signed, *circa* 1891, 21¾in by 18⅛in (55cm by 46cm)
New York $800,000 (£340,426). 12.V.80
From the collection of the late Edgar William and Bernice Chrysler Garbisch

VINCENT VAN GOGH
Le restaurant Rispal à Asnières
1887, 28½in by 23½in (72.5cm by 59.5cm)
New York $790,000 (£336,170). 7.XI.79
From the collection of the Moser family

PAUL SIGNAC
Le port de St Tropez
Signed, inscribed *Op 236* and dated *92*, 25¾in by 31⅞in (65.5cm by 81cm)
New York $490,000(£208,511). 12.V.80
From the collection of the late Edgar William and Bernice Chrysler Garbisch

HENRI EDMOND CROSS
Bormes-la-Jolie
Watercolour and pencil, signed and dated *09*, 8⅝in by 14¾in (22cm by 37.5cm)
London £8,500 ($19,975). 5.XII.79

PAUL SIGNAC
St Tropez
Watercolour and pencil, signed, *circa* 1899, 11in by 14⅜in (28cm by 36.5cm)
London £10,500 ($24,675). 5.XII.79

Opposite
EUGENE BOUDIN
Couple passant devant deux crinolines assises
Watercolour and pencil, stamped with the artist's initials, 6in by 10¼in (15cm by 26cm)
London £12,500 ($29,375). 26.III.80

This watercolour is one of a collection of fifty-four Boudin drawings formed by his friend Léon
Bourgeois, the French politician and Nobel Prizewinner, 1920

PAUL GAUGUIN
Tahitiennes sous les palmiers
Signed and dated *91*, 36¼in by 28¼in (92cm by 71.5cm)
New York $1,800,000 (£765,957). 12.V.80
From the collection of the late Edgar William and Bernice Chrysler Garbisch

PIERRE-AUGUSTE RENOIR
Femme dans un costume oriental
Signed, 1905, 31⅞in by 25¾in (81cm by 65.5cm)
New York $1,000,000 (£425,532). 12.V.80
From the collection of the late Edgar William and Bernice Chrysler Garbisch

ODILON REDON
Fleurs dans un vase brun
Signed, *circa* 1903–1905, 21½in by 18in (54.5cm by 45.5cm)
New York $270,000 (£114,894). 7.XI.79

PIERRE BONNARD
L'heure des bêtes: les chats
Signed, 1906, 29½in by 42½in (75cm by 108cm)
New York $250,000(£106,383). 7.XI.79
From the collection of the Moser family

PAUL CEZANNE
Nature morte: bouilloire, pot-au-lait, sucrier et sept pommes
Watercolour, *circa* 1900–1906, 18¼in by 24¼in (46.5cm by 61.5cm)
London £480,000 ($1,128,000). 1.VII.80

PABLO PICASSO
Carte à jouer, verre, bouteille sur un guéridon
Oil on panel with sand, 1916, $10\frac{5}{8}$in by $13\frac{3}{4}$in (27cm by 35cm)
London £110,000 ($258,500). 1.VII.80

ALBERT GLEIZES
Portrait de Jacques Nayral
Signed and dated *1911*, 71in by 51¼in (180.5cm by 130cm)
London £27,000 ($63,450). 5.XII.79

Jacques Nayral, the playwright, married Gleizes's sister Mireille in 1912. This painting is now in the Tate Gallery

FERNAND LEGER
Les toits de Paris
Signed, 1911, 18in by 15in (45.5cm by 38cm)
London £74,000 ($173,900). 1.VII.80
From the collection of Douglas Cooper

JUAN GRIS
Guitare sur une table
Signed and dated *I-1916*, 36¼in by 23½in (92cm by 59.5cm)
London £135,000 ($317,250). 1.VII.80
From the collection of Douglas Cooper

GEORGES BRAQUE
Guitare, fruits, pipe, cahier de musique
Signed and dated *24*, 46in by 23½in
(117cm by 59.5cm)
London £200,000 ($470,000). 1.VII.80
From the collection of Douglas Cooper

MARC CHAGALL
L'écuyère
Gouache, signed, *circa* 1931, 24¾in by 19in (63cm by 48.5cm)
London £68,000 ($159,800). 26.III.80

LEON BAKST
Costume design for the Firebird
Watercolour, gold paint and pencil, signed, inscribed *oiseau de feu* and dated *1910*,
13¾in by 8½in (35cm by 21.5cm)
London £11,200 ($26,320). 13.III.80

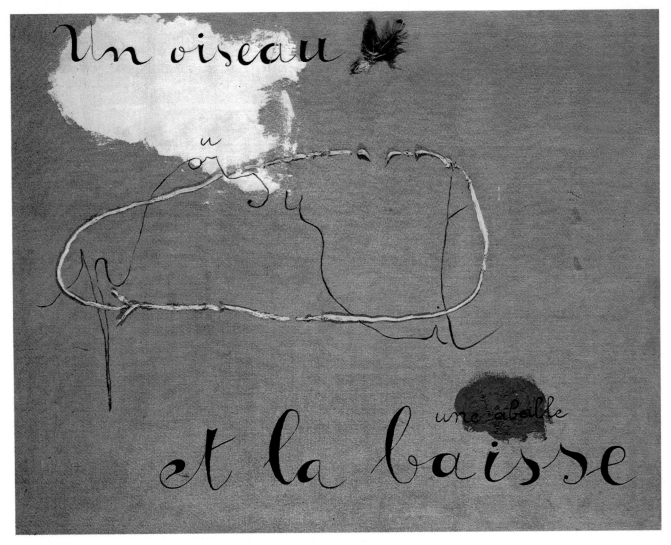

Fig 1
JOAN MIRÓ
Un oiseau poursuit une abeille et la baisse
Oil on canvas with feather, signed and dated *1927*, 32⅞in by 40¼in (83.5cm by 102cm)
New York $330,000 (£140,426). 5.XI.79

Le surréalisme et la peinture: a collection

John Tancock

William N. Copley is an artist who collects, and a collector who paints. In spite of the fact that one great collection was dispersed last November, another of a very different character is being formed, and, as far as his own painting is concerned, business continues as usual. At one point in his life, William Copley was also a dealer. After military service in Africa, Sicily and Italy during the Second World War, Copley began to paint and held his first exhibition at Royer's Bookstore in Los Angeles in 1947. Shortly after, in partnership with his brother-in-law, Copley opened the Copley Galleries in Beverly Hills. It might seem curious that a young painter should have become a dealer so soon after his first exhibition, but in his whimsical memoirs,[1] Copley has provided the explanation. To the painter who signed his pictures CPLY, southern California in 1946 seemed to be an 'intellectual desert'. William Copley, the entrepreneur, decided to introduce California to Surrealism, the most flamboyant literary and pictorial movement of the 1920s and '30s.

Many of the leading figures of the Surrealist movement were in the United States at this time, displaced by the events of the war. Man Ray, who had lived in Paris for many years and was now living in Los Angeles, was offered an exhibition by Copley with ten per cent guaranteed sales at the still unopened gallery. Man Ray gave Copley a letter of introduction to Marcel Duchamp who was then living in New York. Initially Copley was somewhat in awe of 'le Grand Sorcier',[2] a feeling soon overcome by his sense of humour. He came to consider Duchamp his best friend, the latter's position as supreme ironist of the twentieth century serving Copley as an example to be emulated when life became too serious. Duchamp, of course, knew everybody, and introduced Copley to Matta (Echaurren), the most brilliant of the second generation of Surrealists. At Iolas's gallery Copley met the reclusive Joseph Cornell and was greatly impressed with his mysterious and poetic boxes. One final introduction of crucial importance was to Max Ernst, also arranged by Duchamp. After his brief and eventful marriage to Peggy Guggenheim, Ernst moved to Arizona where he was living with the painter Dorothea Tanning.

Thus in a short time Copley had come to know most of the leading Surrealists and those he did not meet before the opening of the gallery, he met soon after, notably Yves Tanguy and René Magritte. In a six-month period he gave exhibitions to René Magritte, Joseph Cornell, Matta, Yves Tanguy, Man Ray and Max Ernst. The Ernst

Fig 2
MAN RAY
A l'heure de l'observatoire: les amoureux
Signed, inscribed with the title and dated *1932–1934*, 39in by 98½in (99cm by 250cm)
New York $750,000 (£319,149). 5.XI.79

exhibition was a major retrospective with more than 300 works from all periods of the artist's activity. An aesthetic triumph the experience may have been, but it was also a financial disaster, and the gallery had to close after six months.

The comically brief career of Copley, the dealer, seems now to have been a vital prelude to his later activities as artist and collector. The Surrealists provided Copley with the fantasy and humour that he deems to be essential to life. With unerring instinct he organised six exhibitions that may not have educated southern California, but certainly provided CPLY, the painter, and William N. Copley, the collector, with a crash course in Surrealism and whetted his appetite. Consequently, in 1951 he moved to Paris until 1963, when he returned to New York. It was during this period that the collection was expanded and refined, assuming more or less the character that it had when it was sold on 5 and 6 November 1979.[3]

The collection was a highly personal one, strongest in the works of those artists to whom Copley was linked by ties of friendship. It was never intended to be nor did it ever become a scholarly survey of all aspects of Dada and Surrealism. For example, the work of Salvador Dali was scarcely represented in the collection. By the time Copley began to collect, Dali was working in his classical manner and thus was of no interest to Copley whose taste is anything but classical. Some of the key works in the collection were acquired right at the beginning. A superlative box by Joseph Cornell, *Soap bubble set, circa* 1947–48, was included in the 1948 exhibition at the Copley Galleries. The rest of the works in the exhibition were given away over the years. Outstanding examples by Man Ray were acquired in 1948, notably *Catherine barometer*, 1920–21, one of the best of the early objects, a chess set of 1920–26, executed in silver for an Indian Prince, and most spectacular of all, *A l'heure de l'observatoire: les amoureux*, 1932–34 (Fig 2). This celebrated image, a fusion in Man Ray's imagination of the luscious lips of Kiki de Montparnasse and Lee Miller, is one of Man Ray's most haunting works, executed with a finesse that he seldom equalled. Beside the

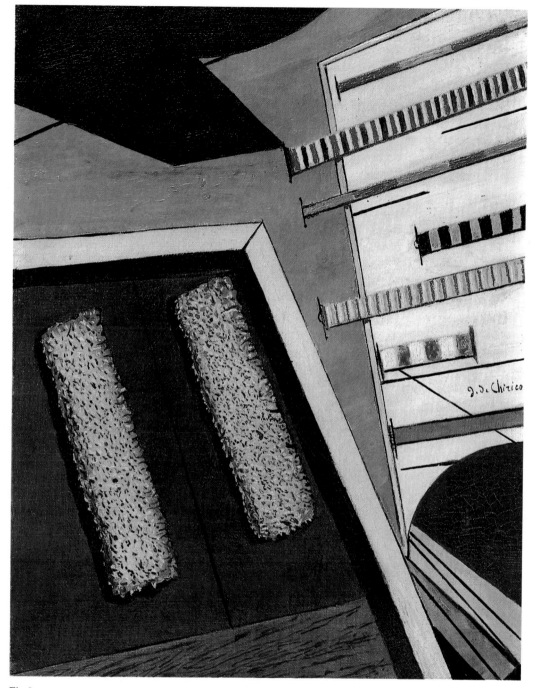

Fig 3
GIORGIO DE CHIRICO
War
Signed, 1916, $13\frac{1}{2}$in by $10\frac{1}{2}$in (34cm by 26.5cm)
New York $170,000 (£72,340). 5.XI.79

giant pair of lips hovering in the sky, Marcel Duchamp's *Pharmacie*, 1914, looked strangely modest. Duchamp's contribution consisted of two small touches of red and green on a cheap commercial print, producing in the process one of the most celebrated Readymades. Of all the Surrealists, Max Ernst was represented most fully in the collection. Several works were acquired in 1948, the little-known *Figure zoomorphe*, 1928, and two major works of the 1940s, *Totem and taboo*, 1941–42, Freudian in title and hallucinatory in the complexity of its technique and imagery, and *Le déjeuner sur l'herbre*, 1944, far removed from Manet and Marcantonio Riamondi.

Thus the nucleus of the collection was formed in the late 1940s. During the 1950s and '60s its strongest areas were consolidated and it also grew in diversity. Jean Arp's *La femme amphore*, a particularly succulent example of the artist's painted wood reliefs, was a major addition in 1952. Two works by Giorgio de Chirico, *War*, 1916 (Fig 3), and a haunting *Study for the portrait of Apollinaire*, which was interpreted as a prediction of the head wound that would cause the poet's death in 1918, introduced the work of one of the most important influences on the Surrealists. *Un oiseau poursuit une abeille et la baisse*, 1927 (Fig 1), by Joan Miró, generally thought to be one of the finest of the calligrammatic *tableau-poèmes* of the 1920s, entered the collection in 1961. Further major additions included three important works by René Magritte, *La chambre d'écoute*, 1953 (Fig 4), *Le sens de la nuit*, 1928, and *Le survivant*, 1950, *Morphologie de l'homme*, 1934, by Victor Brauner, and *Le surréalisme et la peinture*, 1942, by Max Ernst, a summation of Ernst's lifelong obsession with the theme of the bird. On returning to New York in 1963, Copley concentrated on the work of younger contemporary American artists and acquired several outstanding pieces, such as Roy Lichtenstein's *Red painting*, 1965, and Claes Oldenburg's *Soft version of maquette for a monument donated to the city of Chicago by Pablo Picasso*, 1969.

The William N. Copley Collection was the earliest and finest Surrealist collection in America. It was formed intuitively rather than methodically, and for this very reason had a quality that is all but impossible to recapture. The Copley apartment on Central Park West in New York, the last place where it hung as a complete collection, was a remarkably personal achievement, fantastic, bizarre and, above all, humorous. The Surrealists were noted for the ferocity of their internal politics. André Breton, the 'Pope' of the movement, was in the habit of expelling members and new alliances were constantly being formed. As reassembled by Copley, old grievances were forgotten and the leading figures of the group, represented by superior examples of their work, lived in perfect harmony. It was a monument to a lost period in European history when fantasy took precedence over logic and poetry reigned supreme.

[1] William N. Copley, *Portrait de l'Artiste en Jeune Marchand de Tableau* (Paris/New York, Centre National d'art et de culture Georges Pompidou, Musée National d'art moderne, 1 June – 19 September 1977), pp 89–105

[2] *Ibid*, p 94

[3] Several important works from the collection had already been sold at Sotheby Parke Bernet, New York on 17 May 1978, notably *La trahison des images* by René Magritte (now in the Los Angeles County Museum of Art), *L'évidence éternelle*, 1930, by René Magritte and *La porte (objet)*, 1931, by Joan Miró. *La nuit éspagnole*, 1922, by Francis Picabia was sold privately and is now in the collection of Dr Peter Ludwig, Cologne.

Fig 4
RENE MAGRITTE
La chambre d'écoute
Signed, 1953, 31¼in by 39in (79.5cm by 99cm)
New York $270,000 (£114,894). 5.XI.79

MAX ERNST
Le surréalisme et la peinture
Signed and dated *1942*, 76¾in by 91¾in (195cm by 233cm)
New York $620,000 (£263,830). 5.XI.79
From the collection of William N. Copley

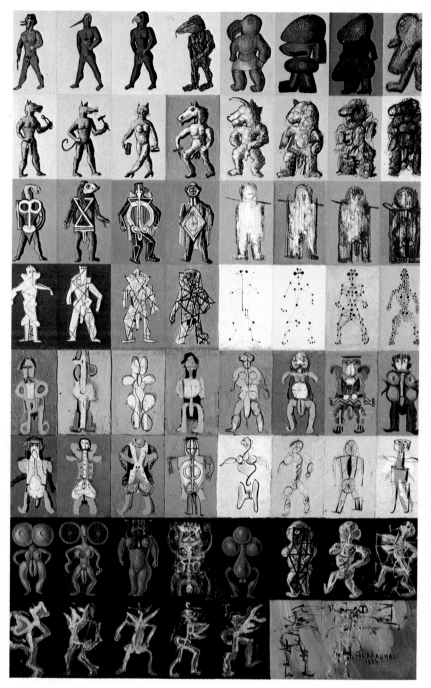

VICTOR BRAUNER
Morphologie de l'homme
Signed and dated *1934*, 70in by 45⅝in (178cm by 116cm)
New York $130,000(£55,319). 5.XI.79
From the collection of William N. Copley

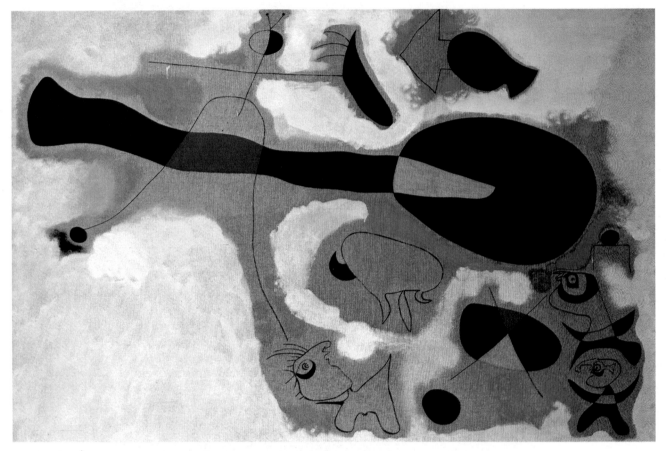

JOAN MIRÓ
Jeune fille moitié brune moitié rousse glissant sur le sang des jacinthes gelées d'un camp de football en
flammes
Signed, inscribed with the title and dated *14–III–939* on the reverse, 51in by 76½in
(129.5cm by 194.5cm)
New York $400,000 (£170,213). 14.V.80

YVES TANGUY
Il y a
Signed and dated '47, 50in by 39¾in (127cm by 101cm)
New York $270,000 (£114,894). 5.XI.79
From the collection of William N. Copley

EMILE-ANTOINE BOURDELLE
Grande Pénélope no. 1
Bronze, signed, inscribed *Alexis Rudier Fondeur Paris*, with a Greek inscription (Penelope waiting for Ulysses), and dated *1912*, height 96¾in (246cm)
Monte Carlo FF 580,000 (£59,794:$140,516). 25.XI.79

AUGUSTE RODIN
Jean d'Aire, nu pour le monument Les bourgeois de Calais
Bronze, signed and inscribed *Alexis Rudier Fondeur Paris, circa* 1886, height 80in (203cm)
Monte Carlo FF 1,050,000 (£108,247:$254,381). 25.XI.79

AUGUSTE RODIN
L'appel aux armes (*La défense*)
Bronze, signed and inscribed *Alexis Rudier Fondeur Paris*, 1878–79, height $44\frac{1}{2}$in (113cm)
Monte Carlo FF 480,000 (£49,485; $116,289). 25.XI.79

MAX ERNST
Oiseau
Wood, *circa* 1924, height 40in (101.5cm)
London £43,000 ($101,050). 5.XII.79

CONSTANTIN BRANCUSI
Head
Wood, *circa* 1919–23, height 12in (30.5cm)
London £60,000($141,000). 26.III.80

This is the head of the sculpture *Plato* which was removed from
the rest of the figure *circa* 1923. The main body of the sculpture,
also known as *Little French girl II*, was subsequently destroyed
by Brancusi. This sculpture is now in the Tate Gallery

HENRY MOORE, OM, CH
Two piece sculpture no. 10: Interlocking
Bronze, signed and numbered 6/7, 1968, length 36in (91.5cm)
London £32,000 ($75,200). 1.VII.80

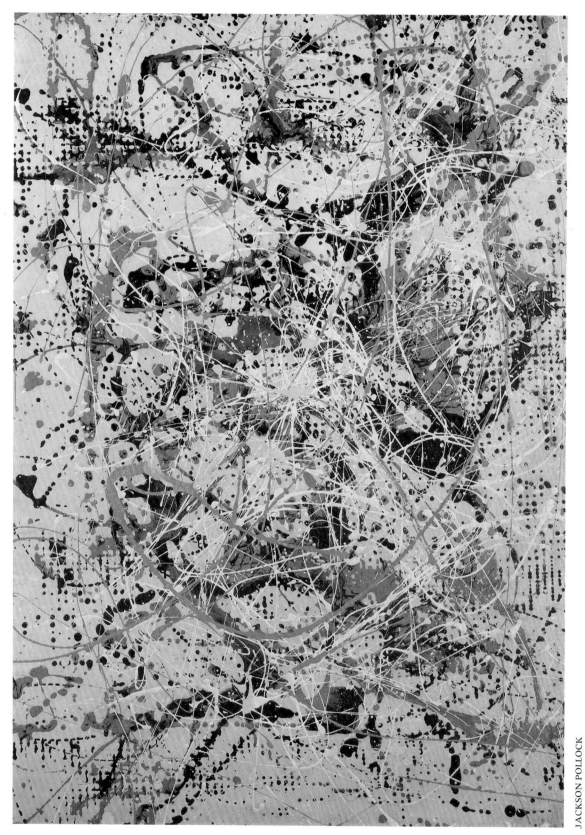

JACKSON POLLOCK
Painting no. 21
On paper, signed and dated 49, $19\frac{1}{4}$in by $27\frac{1}{2}$in (49.5cm by 70cm)
London £70,000($164,500). 5.XII.79

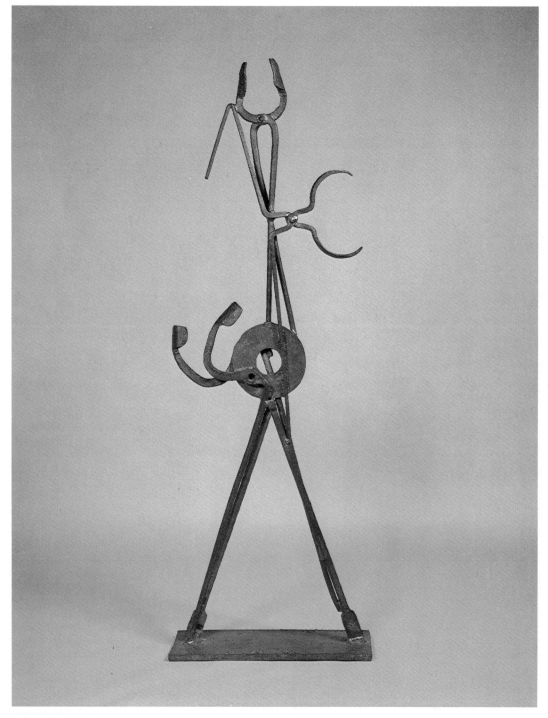

DAVID SMITH
Voltri XX
Steel, signed, inscribed with the title and numbered *6–62* on the base, height $77\frac{3}{4}$in (197.5cm)
New York $135,000 (£57,447). 8.XI.79

DAVID HOCKNEY
Some neat cushions
Acrylic, 1967, 62in square (157.5cm square)
New York $60,000 (£25,532). 15.V.80
From the collection of Carter Burden

ROY LICHTENSTEIN
Oh, Jeff . . . I love you, too . . . but . . .
Acrylic, signed and dated '64 on the reverse, 48in square (122cm square)
New York $210,000 (£89,362). 15.V.80
From the collection of the Abrams family

FRANCIS BACON
From Muybridge – studies of the human body – woman emptying a bowl of water, and paralytic child on all fours
Signed on the reverse, 1965, 78in by 58in (198cm by 147.5cm)
New York $180,000 (£76,596). 15.V.80

CHRISTO
Large store front
Mixed media on wood with electric light, signed, inscribed and dated *64*, 63in by 49½in
(160cm by 125.5cm)
London £19,000 ($44,650). 5.XII.79

EDWARD HICKS
The peaceable kingdom
Circa 1844–45, 24in by 31¼in (61cm by 79.5cm)
New York $270,000 (£114,894). 30.IV.80
From the collection of the late Leonardo L. Beans

MARTIN JOHNSON HEADE
Sailing off the coast
Signed and dated *1869*, 15in by 29in (38cm by 73.5cm)
New York $75,000 (£31,915). 25.IV.80

JOHN GEORGE BROWN
The sidewalk dance
Signed and dated *copyright 1894*, with the J. G. Brown Sale stamp on the reverse, $40\frac{1}{4}$in by 60in
(102cm by 152.5cm)
New York $105,000 (£44,681). 25.IV.80

ALBERT BIERSTADT
Indian encampment, late afternoon
Signed and dated *1862*, 20in by 28in (51cm by 71cm)
New York $300,000 (£127,660). 25.IV.80

Fig 1
FREDERIC EDWIN CHURCH
The icebergs
Signed and dated *1861*, 64¼in by 112¼in (163cm by 285cm)
New York $2,500,000 (£1,063,830). 25.X.79
From the collection of the Social Services Department, City of Manchester

American paintings in Europe

James Miller

In June 1979, after a century of obscurity, Frederic Edwin Church's *The icebergs* (Fig 1) was found in Manchester. Its rediscovery in England immediately begs certain questions as to why it was here, and why it had remained hidden for so long. In 1863, Frederic Church decided to bring his painting of *The icebergs* to London, where it was heralded as one of the most important pictures seen during that season, and even as late as 1869 an English critic noted that it was 'the most astonishing tour de force ever executed on canvas'. Between 1857 and 1869, Church had organised nine exhibitions of his major works in London to establish his reputation in Europe. These displays increased both his international prestige and his earnings from the pictures on view – entrance fees were charged and reproductive prints were subsequently sold.

After the 1863 exhibition *The icebergs* was purchased anonymously by Sir Edward Watkin (1819–1901). Sir Edward was a northern businessman and railway magnate, who became a leading Liberal politician: his interest in trade, especially with America, led him to head the commission that bought the Hudson Bay Company for the British Government in the 1870s. The painting was hung in Sir Edward's country seat, Rose Hill, outside Manchester, where it remained even after his descendants had sold the property at the turn of the century. Indeed, at that time it would appear that the large dark canvas, known as *The wreck*, was unrecognised as a picture of any importance, and passed with the contents of the house to the new owners. During the first decades of this century, the house became a convalescent home and was eventually administered by the City of Manchester itself.

The picture remained at Rose Hill until 1979, when it was decided to redecorate the hall. Once the large painting was taken down, it was generally felt that the staircase looked much better without its ominous shadow. Expert advice was consulted in order to identify the work and to discover whether the painting was of any value. Because the subject of *The icebergs* was still known from the contemporary prints, it was relatively easy to establish that this was Church's missing masterpiece, and due to the general lack of interest shown in the picture over the years, it had remained in good condition: even its original frame was discovered in a wood shed behind the house. When the deeply discoloured varnish was removed the painting's true luminous colours of ice green and translucent blue, which had been only dimly visible for so many years, were revealed. W. P. B. Bailey's seemingly excessive praise of Church in the *Art Journal* as 'no less than a successor to J. M. W. Turner' was once again understandable.

The rediscovery of this painting underlines a fact which recently has become more apparent – because of the desire to establish a reputation in Europe during the nineteenth century, American artists brought their paintings to London and other European capitals to demonstrate their skill. After these exhibitions their pictures were quite often sold to patrons in those countries, and, indeed, even Queen Victoria commissioned a work from William Bradford.

Bradford (1827–92) visited England ten years after Church, and organised an exhibition of his pictures in the Langham Hotel in the summer of 1873. Included in this show was another painting that has recently come to light, *The wreck of an emigrant ship on the coast of New England*. The artist had been working on this subject during the 1860s and after its exhibition in London it must have found a purchaser. It re-emerged in a house in the Midlands last autumn, and was subsequently included in a sale of topographical paintings in London last February. In the same sale was a painting of *Winter in Pennsylvania – a party in a horse-drawn sledge leaving a village* by the Philadelphia artist Thomas Birch and dated *1833*. This, too, had been in an English collection but was thought to have been a view in Surrey.

Another aspect of British patrons' interest in American nineteenth-century art was their fascination with the American Indian and the exploration of the West. In the early 1960s, a group of watercolours by Alfred Jacob Miller depicting the American fur trade of the 1830s, which had descended through his English family, were rediscovered, and one of the first sales at Parke-Bernet in New York was devoted to these. More recently, in September 1978, a particularly fine and unrecorded water-colour by Charles Marion Russell called *After his first hunt* (see *Art at Auction 1978–79*, p 142) emerged from a collection in the north of England, and last March a previously unrecorded watercolour of finches by the Anglo-American artist John James Audubon (Fig 2) was sold in London. Audubon had visited Prideaux John Selby, the English ornithologist, in Northumberland in 1827, and had painted this watercolour for Mrs Selby to commemorate his stay at their house at Twizell. Audubon actually noted in his journals that he and Mrs Selby's brother Captain Mitford went out and shot the birds and then Audubon drew them as a present. This rare watercolour had remained in the Selby family ever since, and was remarkably fresh and unfaded.

Whilst these paintings, and especially the Church, represent some of the more spectacular rediscoveries in the last few years, scarcely a week goes by in London without some missing or unrecorded American or Canadian painting surfacing. It is certainly evident from the records left in the nineteenth century, that there are a large number of lost paintings from that continent still to be found.

Fig 2 (*opposite*)
JOHN JAMES AUDUBON
A chaffinch, bullfinch and greenfinch on a branch of budding chestnuts
Pen and black ink, watercolour and bodycolour on wove, inscribed *To Mrs. Lewis Selby from her grateful and most obedient servant John J. Audubon* and dated *Twizell April 10th 1827*,
$14\frac{3}{4}$ in by $10\frac{3}{4}$ in (37.5cm by 27.5cm)
London £51,000 ($119,850). 13.III.80
From the collection of the late Sir Geoffrey Selby Church

ARTHUR FITZWILLIAM TAIT
The check – keep your distance
Signed and dated *N.Y.52*, 30in by 44in (76cm by 112cm)
Los Angeles $200,000 (£85,106). 24.VI.80
From the collection of Liz Whitney Tippett

CHARLES MARION RUSSELL
Crees coming in to trade
Watercolour, signed and with skull device, dated *1896*, and inscribed with the title on the reverse,
19¾in by 28¼in (50cm by 72cm)
New York $155,000 (£65,957). 25.X.79

THEODORE ROBINSON
Stepping stones
1893, 21½in by 28½in (54.5cm by 72.5cm)
New York $120,000 (£51,064). 25.X.79

The two girls depicted in this painting are the daughters of J. H. Twachtman

FREDERICK CHILDE HASSAM
Union Square
Signed and dated *N.Y. 1892*, 18in by 15in (46cm by 38cm)
New York $190,000 (£80,851). 25.IV.80
From the collection of the late Mabel Brady Garvan

WINSLOW HOMER
Orange trees and gate
Watercolour, signed and dated *1885*, 14¼in by 20¾in (36cm by 52.5cm)
New York $165,000 (£70,213). 25.IV.80
From the collection of the late Priscilla Alden Bartlett Henderson

EDWARD HOPPER
The lee shore
Signed, 1941, 28$\frac{1}{4}$in by 43in (71.5cm by 109.5cm)
New York $230,000 (£97,872). 25.X.79
From the collection of the Sara Roby Foundation

JOHN SLOAN
Spring planting, Greenwich Village, N.Y.C.
Signed, signed and inscribed with the title on the reverse, 1913, 26in by 32in (66cm by 81.5cm)
New York $130,000 (£55,319). 25.IV.80
From the collection of the late Mrs Cyrus McCormick

WIFREDO LAM
Eggue Orissi, la hierba de los dioses
Signed and dated *1943*, 71½in by 49in (181.5cm by 124.5cm)
New York $95,000 (£40,426). 17.X.79

RUFINO TAMAYO
Hombre con sandía
Signed and dated *49*, 39¼in by 31⅝in (99.5cm by 80.5cm)
New York $125,000 (£53,191). 9.V.80

HECTOR HYPPOLITE
Voodoo purification ceremony
Enamel on masonite, signed and inscribed, *circa* 1948, 47in by 34in (119.5cm by 86.5cm)
PB Eighty-four $28,000 (£11,915). 6.V.80
From the collection of Mrs John Train

CORNELIUS KRIEGHOFF
Indian hunters resting by a campfire
Signed, mid nineteenth century, 25in by 43in (63.5cm by 109.5cm)
Toronto Can $140,000 (£51,852:$121,852). 27.V.80

FREDERICK HORSMAN VARLEY, ARCA
Summer in the Arctic
Signed and inscribed with the title on the reverse, *circa* 1939, 34in by 40in (86.5cm by 101.5cm)
Toronto Can $170,000 (£62,963:$147,963). 27.V.80

ALTO PERU, EIGHTEENTH CENTURY
The Archangel Salamiel
Inscribed *Salamiel*, 63in by 41¼in (160cm by 105cm)
New York $27,000 (£11,489). 9.V.80

This style of ceremonial portrait of an angel bearing arms is unique to northern Peru.
The costume and musket derive from the Netherlands

Prints

MARTIN SCHONGAUER
The signs of the four Evangelists
One of a set of four engravings, late 1480s, diameter approximately 3⅜in (8.5cm)
New York $19,000 (£8,085). 15.II.80

ERICH HECKEL
Zwei ruhende Frauen
Woodcut, the second state of three, signed and dated *1909*, $12\frac{3}{4}$in by $14\frac{3}{4}$in (32.5cm by 37.5cm)
New York $45,000 (£19,149). 13.II.80

EMIL NOLDE
Freihafen Hamburg
Woodcut on wove, the first state of two, signed and inscribed *Freihafen Hamburg herzlichst Herrn*
Sadleir gewidmet von., 1910, 11¾in by 15½in (30cm by 39.5cm)
London £3,600 ($8,460). 17.V.80

PAUL GAUGUIN
· *Manao tupapau*
 Woodcut on japan paper, 1894, $8\frac{7}{8}$in by $14\frac{7}{8}$in (22.5cm by 38cm)
 London £27,000 ($63,450). 26.XI.79

EDVARD MUNCH
Zwei Menschen – die Einsamen
Woodcut on simili-japan paper, the first state of three, signed, 1899, $15\frac{1}{2}$in by $21\frac{7}{8}$in
(39.5cm by 55.5cm)
London £45,000 ($105,750). 26.XI.79

HENRI DE TOULOUSE–LAUTREC
Eldorado: Aristide Bruant
Lithograph, 1892, 53$\frac{7}{8}$in by 37$\frac{5}{8}$in (137cm by 95.5cm)
New York $26,000 (£11,064). 12.XII.79

HENRI DE TOULOUSE-LAUTREC
Aux Ambassadeurs
Lithograph on wove, the second state, signed, 1894, $11\frac{5}{8}$in by $9\frac{1}{2}$in (29.5cm by 24cm)
London £11,000 ($25,850). 16.V.80

Fig 1
Woman bathing (*La toilette*)
Drypoint and aquatint, fifth and final state, proof outside the edition, signed with
initials, 1891, 14$\frac{3}{8}$in by 10$\frac{1}{2}$in (36.5cm by 26.5cm)
New York $72,000 (£30,638). 14.II.80

Mary Cassatt's innovative technique

Adelyn D. Breeskin

In examining the technical development of Mary Cassatt's graphic work, it is obvious that from her fifth print onwards she stressed the use of soft-ground etching. She continued using soft-ground – sometimes with aquatint, a few times with etching, but mostly alone – to her thirty-fourth plate, in which she experimented with a varied combination of soft-ground, aquatint, etching and drypoint, and even introduced the use of fabric texture. In 1879, Degas invited Cassatt to join him and Camille Pissarro in producing original prints for publication in a journal to be called *Le Jour et La Nuit*. This enterprise, he insisted, would teach them all to draw. The journal never materialised, but the prints that Cassatt prepared for it started her on her extensive graphic career. It was for the never-realised journal that she completed not only her twenty-second plate, *In the opera box, no.3*, in soft-ground touched up with aquatint, but also the above-mentioned thirty-fourth plate, called *The visitor*. In a letter to Pissarro, Degas mentioned that she was at this time making 'some delightful graphic experiments'. Her use in *The visitor* of twill fabric, pressed into soft-ground and combined with a full gamut of other graphic media, must certainly be accounted a bold innovation for the time.

After completing these and other major works mostly in soft-ground, Cassatt turned to drypoint, and her preference for this medium soon asserted itself. She often mixed her drypoint with soft-ground and sometimes with netting texture. The culmination of the series of twelve drypoints was published in an edition of twenty-five of each, first shown in 1893 in her large one-person exhibition at Durand-Ruel's in Paris and, two years later in Durand-Ruel's New York branch. Aside from this published series and one other series mentioned below (as well as fifty prints of *In the opera box, no.3* and twenty-five of two other prints – *Preparing Bill for an outing* and *Nurse and baby Bill, no.2*), all of the early prints seem to have been limited to only four or five impressions. Many of them were made on the backs of copper plates as well as on the fronts, an indication that she was engaging in experimental practice rather than in the production of finished works of art.

In 1891, Cassatt learned that the Société des Peintures-Graveurs Français was planning an exhibition from which both she and Pissarro were to be excluded, since neither of them was born in France. Angered, she persuaded Pissarro to join her in engaging a gallery at Durand-Ruel adjoining those to be used by the Société. She then set to work to produce a series of ten colour prints. When all three shows opened, these colour prints were found to surpass the work of the Société's members. The

Fig 2
The fitting
Drypoint and soft-ground, final state, proof outside the edition, signed and with
the artist's monogram stamp, 1891, 14¾in by 10in (37.5cm by 25.5cm)
New York $38,000 (£16,170). 14.II.80

Fig 3
Afternoon tea party
Drypoint, soft-ground and aquatint, final state, trial proof outside the edition, signed
with initials, 1891, $13\frac{5}{8}$in by $10\frac{1}{2}$in (34.5cm by 26.5cm)
New York $37,000 (£15,745). 14.II.80

Japanese exhibition shown at the Ecole des Beaux-Arts during 1890 had deeply impressed Cassatt, and in her colour prints she imitated the viewpoint taken by Japanese printmakers. Translating their woodcut techniques into her preferred medium, she worked in drypoint over soft-ground, sometimes heightened with aquatint. In this arduous undertaking she was assisted by a printer named LeRoy; the two of them, she wrote, after working for a stint of eight hours, would often finish only eight impressions. The resulting ten colour prints (eg Figs 1–4) proved to be such a triumph that they would give Mary Cassatt a just claim to fame if they were her only accomplishment. Upon seeing the finest of them, *Woman bathing* (Fig 1), Degas exclaimed that he would not admit that a woman could draw that well. Such draughtsmanship is indeed masterly. It was done directly from the model on paper wrapped over a copper plate prepared with soft-ground. Wherever a line or a tone had been drawn, the soft-ground adhered to the paper and came off with it, leaving the lines of copper plate exposed. The plate was then placed in an acid bath to be lightly bitten. The etched soft-ground line became the guide for drypoint lines and for drypoint as well as soft-ground tonal areas. This process was repeated on one or two other plates for each of the colour prints.

The problems of printing in colour demanded full consideration of the surface to be printed. Since soft-ground tonal areas have a flatness that might be considered monotonous and thin if unrelieved, Cassatt sometimes added aquatint to enrich the tone. Wiping a plate thoroughly over aquatint, however, can result in a discolouring of the ink. On the other hand, soft-ground leaves a good, clear surface to be wiped. The complicated printing that Cassatt evolved came about because soft-ground allowed it: the etched plate, especially in light tones, retains a strong, smooth surface on which to wipe, broken by tiny pits that hold the ink. In contrast, aquatint produces a bumpy surface, and, what with the discolouration of ink, would have been somewhat cumbersome and unsatisfactory.

Why then did Cassatt entitle this great series of her colour prints *Série de dix planches/pointe sèche et aquatinte/impressions en couleurs*? Because she stressed aquatint and did not even mention soft-ground, these prints have always been known as 'coloured aquatints'. My opinion is that she preferred to keep her technical facility in the use of soft-ground from being generally exploited. In 1891, soft-ground was a very innovative method and Cassatt devoted years of trial and error in perfecting her use of the medium. Soft-ground had first been used during the second half of the eighteenth century and into the first half of the nineteenth. Gainsborough and Cotman had used it, as well as a few other English artists. After Cassatt's experiments toward the end of the last century, the possibilities of soft-ground were not fully explored until Jacques Villon turned to it. Like Cassatt, Villon both had expert knowledge of his *métier* and could draw on a remarkable reservoir of inventiveness and imagination. Through his work in soft-ground at Stanley William Hayter's 'Atelier 17', Villon's methods were introduced into the United States in 1940. Today, the soft-ground textures employed by Cassatt in Paris before 1880 are used by printmakers throughout the world. We can therefore, with justification, place Mary Cassatt as a nineteenth-century graphic artist who was about one hundred years ahead of her time.

Fig 4
In the omnibus (*In the tramway*)
Drypoint and soft-ground, the third state of four, signed with initials, 1891,
$14\frac{3}{8}$in by $10\frac{1}{2}$in (36.5cm by 26.5cm)
New York $39,000 (£16,596). 14.II.80

LASZLO MOHOLY-NAGY
Kestnermappe Konstruktionen 6
One of a set of six lithographs, signed, 1923, 23⅝in by 17⅜in
(60cm by 44cm)
Los Angeles $26,000 (£11,064). 18.VI.80

JASPER JOHNS
Untitled
Lithograph, signed, numbered *46/53* and dated '77, $24\frac{3}{4}$in by $35\frac{3}{8}$in (63cm by 90cm)
New York $6,300 (£2,681). 19.X.79

L. EKEMAN-ALLESSON, after RUDOLF KUNST
Chevaux de races orientales aux haras de S.M. le Roi de Wurttemberg
One of a set of eighteen lithographs, published 1823, oblong folio
London £6,500 ($15,275). 29.V.80

L. Ekeman-Allesson was appointed by the King of Wurttemberg Professor and Director of
the Royal Institute of Lithography, Stuttgart, where these lithographs were printed

ALEXANDER ORLOWSKI
A Persian on horseback
Chalk-lithograph, proof before title, 1819,
$20\frac{5}{8}$in by $16\frac{1}{4}$in (52.5cm by 41.5cm)
London £320 ($752). 27.XI.79

THOMAS ROWLANDSON
Amputation
Coloured etching and aquatint, published October 1793, $11\frac{5}{8}$in by $15\frac{7}{8}$in
(29.5cm by 40.5cm)
London £600 ($1,410). 29.V.80
From the collection of A. K. T. Boedinghaus

ALBRECHT DÜRER
The Passion
One of a set of sixteen engravings, 1509–
1513, approximately $4\frac{5}{8}$in by $2\frac{7}{8}$in
(12cm by 7.5cm)
London £13,500 ($31,725). 16.V.80

PIETER VAN DER HEYDEN, after HIERONYMUS BOSCH
Die blau Schuÿte
Engraving, 1559, $8\frac{7}{8}$in by $11\frac{3}{4}$in (22.5cm by 30cm)
London £5,800 ($13,630). 28.XI.79

This impression is a previously unrecorded first state before the correction
of the title

ADRIAEN VAN OSTADE
The breakfast
Etching, the fourth state of twelve, *circa* 1664, 8⅝in by 10¼in (22cm by 26cm)
New York $30,000 (£12,766). 15.II.80

REMBRANDT HARMENSZ. VAN RIJN
Self portrait wearing a cap
Etching, *circa* 1634, 2in by 1¾in
(5cm by 4.5cm)
London £18,500 ($43,475). 16.V.80

REMBRANDT HARMENSZ. VAN RIJN
Self portrait wearing a cap, open mouthed
Etching, 1630, 2in by 1¾in (5cm by 4.5cm)
New York $17,000 (£7,234). 15.II.80

REMBRANDT HARMENSZ. VAN RIJN
The little Jewish bride (*Saskia as
St Catherine*)
Etching, 1638, 4⅜in by 3in
(11cm by 7.5cm)
London £13,000 ($30,550). 16.V.80

REMBRANDT HARMENSZ. VAN RIJN
Three etchings from the *Recueil de quatre-vingt-cinq estampes originals*, as published by
Pierre-François Basan, *circa* 1789–97, folio
London £45,000 ($105,750). 16.V.80

This volume is one of three known extant copies of the P.-F. Basan edition

GIOVANNI BATTISTA TIEPOLO
Vari capricci
One of a set of ten etchings, executed *circa* 1743, approximately 5⅜in by 7⅛in (13.5cm by 18cm)
London £10,250($24,088). 28.XI.79

Manuscripts and Printed Books

Krishna in pursuit of the bull demon, a north Indian miniature from the *Bhagavata Purana, circa* 1540–60
New York $2,600 (£1,106). 14.XII.79

RASHID AL-DIN
Jami' al-Tawarikh (World History), an Arabic manuscript, illustrated with 100 miniatures, dated *AH 714* (1314 AD), Tabriz
London £850,000 ($1,997,500). 8.VII.80
From the collection of the Royal Asiatic Society of Great Britain and Ireland

Rashid al-Din's *World History*

Toby Falk

The creation of the greatest illustrated manuscripts is invariably a combined effort by several personalities with strength of character and originality of approach. This is borne out by the *Jami' al-Tawarikh* or *World History*, commissioned by the Il-Khanid ruler of Tabriz, Uljaytu (reigned 1304–16), and written and compiled by his court historian Rashid al-Din.

Rashid al-Din, the son of an apothecary, was a man of extraordinary energy and ability, who trained as a physician and rose to the position of vizier at the Il-Khanid court. One of his duties was to design the new suburb of Rashidiya on the hillside to the east of Tabriz, where many of the important public buildings necessary for the newly expanded capital could be situated. In addition to the mosques, offices, schools and palaces was the scriptorium, a centre which brought together the scholars – astronomers, physicians, calligraphers, historians, theologians and mathematicians – who participated in intellectual projects and wrote works for Uljaytu's library. Most of the manuscripts from Rashid al-Din's scriptorium have since disappeared, but one of the most ambitious and far reaching was his *World History*, of which only two parts survive. In its entirety, this up-dated compilation of all the written and oral knowledge available to Mongol historians would have run to numerous volumes, prepared in both Persian and Arabic. Rashid al-Din brought together men of many nationalities and skills to cover the wide spectrum of subjects: in addition to histories of China, India, Iran and the Mongols, there were accounts of the background of Islam, Buddhism and the Jews. Rashid al-Din lived to be over seventy, but his work was curtailed by political intrigue when he was deposed and executed in 1318.

Present-day interest in the manuscript volumes lies mainly with the illustrations. Settled after the disruptions of the Mongol invasions fifty years earlier, Il-Khanid Tabriz was a magnetic centre of cultural activity attracting artists from far afield. The pictorial result in the *World History* was a remarkable combination of stylistic techniques, salted with a fresh and straightforward vigour. The rendering of Noah and his Ark (folio 48r; see opposite) is based upon a ship of Byzantine origin, while for the mountains between India and Tibet we are given a distinctly Chinese landscape inhabited by Tibetan and Indian figures. It is this fusion of iconographic elements which has given the illustrations of the manuscript their peculiar strength. Their subsequent importance was as a foundation stone for the art of miniature painting in Persia, which flourished over the next four centuries, reaching its ultimate development under the Timurids and Safavids.

The Qur'an, an illuminated leaf in eastern kufic script, Iraq or Persia, eleventh century
London £5,500 ($12,925). 8.VII.80

RIZA-I ABBASI
Portrait of a pensive youth, a Persian miniature, signed, Isfahan, early
seventeenth century
London £14,000 ($32,900). 21.IV.80
From the collection of the Hagop Kevorkian Fund

A princess choosing jewellery from a display presented by her hand-maidens at night, an
Indian miniature, Kangra, *circa* 1800–1810
London £6,500 ($15,275). 7.VII.80

Six of Colonel Skinner's young recruits standing in a row, watercolour, Punjab or Himalayas, *circa* 1815–19
London £7,200 ($16,920). 7.VII.80
From the collection of Malcolm R. Fraser

This Company school drawing is one of a group of forty-five watercolours executed, probably by Ghulam 'Ali Khan, during William Fraser's expedition to the Himalayas, 1815–19

The Yorkshire Apocalypse, a manuscript in Latin and French rhyming verse, with ninety-four half-page miniatures, written by the scribe John of Parlington in Yorkshire, *circa* 1310–25 London £52,000 ($122,200). 24.VI.80

This is a previously unrecorded illustrated manuscript

Hours of the Virgin, a Dutch decorated manuscript on vellum, northern
Netherlands, probably Utrecht, 1490
London £40,000 ($94,000). 11.XII.79

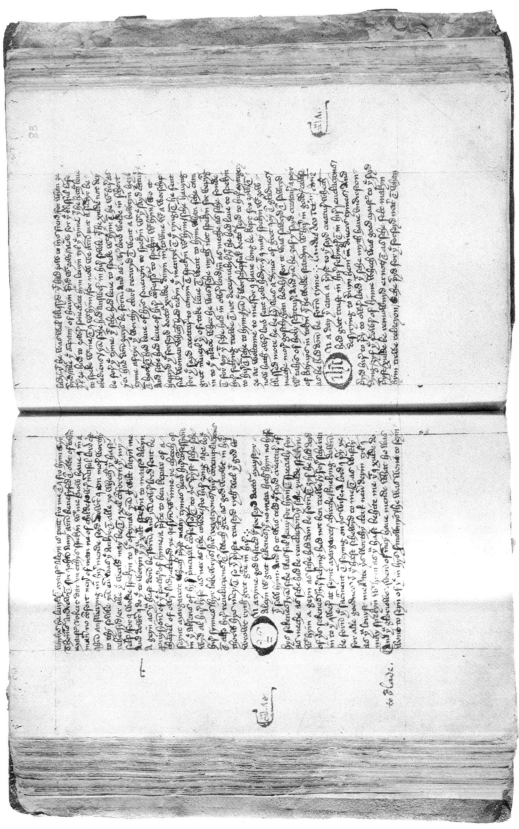

The Book of Margery Kempe, a Middle English manuscript, East Anglia, probably King's Lynn, *circa* 1440
London £50,000 ($117,500). 24.VI.80
From the collection of Capt. M.E. Butler-Bowdon

This is the oldest known English autobiography and the only known manuscript of this text

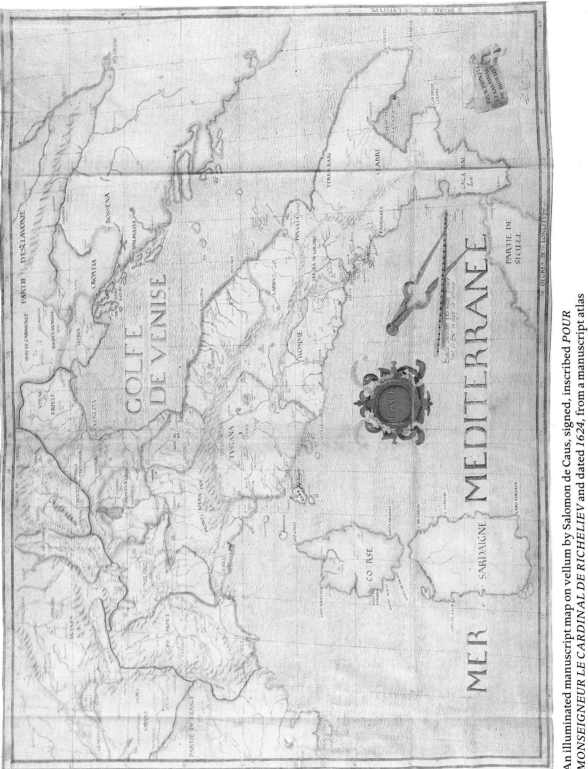

An illuminated manuscript map on vellum by Salomon de Caus, signed, inscribed *POUR MONSEIGNEUR LE CARDINAL DE RICHELIEV* and dated *1624*, from a manuscript atlas comprising fifty-eight charts, maps and plans of Spain and Spanish-held territory in the Mediterranean, *circa* 1624–40

London £16,000 ($37,600). 30.VI.80

The farm accounts of Ely Abbey, an Anglo-Saxon manuscript on vellum, *circa* 1007–1025
London £52,000 ($122,200). 11.XII.79
From the collection of Queens' College, Cambridge

ALFRED LORD TENNYSON
An autograph manuscript of *In Memoriam*, written in a 'long, butcher-ledger-like book', *circa* 1842
London £100,000 ($235,000). 22.VII.80
From the collection of the Tennyson Trust

This is the most complete autograph manuscript of Tennyson's celebrated poem

HENRY VIII
An initial letter portrait of Henry VIII
from a Royal Letters Patent, on vellum,
with the Great Seal of England,
Westminster, 22 February 1538
London £2,800 ($6,580). 17.XII.79

ELIZABETH I
A signed letter, with an autograph docket by Lord
Burghley, countersigned by Robert Cecil and the Earl of
Essex, giving authority to Charles, Lord Howard of
Effingham, and Robert, Earl of Essex, to muster a fleet and
an army to resist the threat of the Spanish Armada of 1596,
18 March 1596
London £6,200 ($14,570). 17.XII.79

HENRY VIII
A signed letter to Cosimo I de' Medici, Duke of Florence, introducing his
servant Ludovico Da l'Armi, Westminster, 16 February 1545
London £6,000 ($14,100). 2.VI.80
From the collection of the late R.E.D. Rawlins

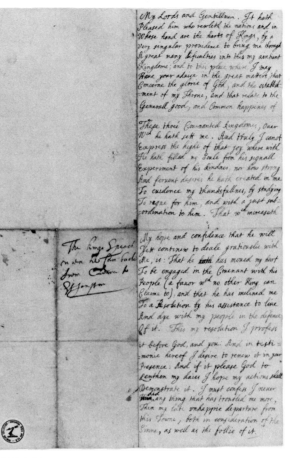

CHARLES II

An autograph speech delivered as an apology to the
Covenanters, after the failure of Charles's attempted
escape from Perth known as 'the Start', October 1650
London £3,400 ($7,990). 2.VI.80
From the collection of the late R.E.D. Rawlins

CHARLES I

An autograph letter to his nephew Prince Rupert of the
Rhine, reproaching him for surrendering Bristol to
Sir Thomas Fairfax, Hereford, 14 September 1645
London £6,600 ($15,510). 21.VII.80
From the collection of the late Col. Alan Gandar Dower

AUGUSTUS JOHN, OM, RA
The archive of his letters, manuscripts and
sketch-books, *circa* 1900–1961
London £52,000 ($122,200). 17.XII.79
From the collection of the John family

G. E. MOORE, OM
The archive of his philosophical papers, lecture
notes, diaries, correspondence, personal papers
and books from his library, *circa* 1882–1958
London £48,000 ($112,800). 17.XII.79
From the collection of Timothy Moore

EZRA POUND
Authorial typescripts, with autograph revisions, of sixteen Cantos including the
complete *Fifth Decad of Cantos, circa* 1937
London £11,000 ($25,850). 22.VII.80

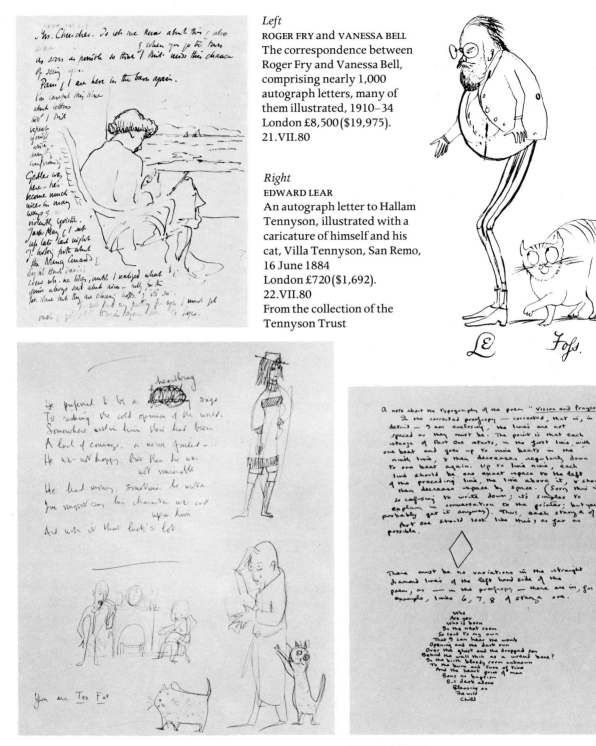

MARTIN LUTHER
An autograph letter to his protector
the Elector John Frederick of Saxony,
pleading for his intervention on
behalf of Wolfgang Newer,
Wittenberg, 1 December 1538
London £13,000 ($30,550). 29.IV.80

JEAN-JACQUES ROUSSEAU
Herbarium, containing over 400 samples of
plants and flowers, with autograph notes,
circa 1765–72
London £7,500 ($17,625). 20.XI.79

RICHARD WAGNER
An autograph letter to Liszt's secretary Belloni, written shortly after Wagner's
banishment from Dresden, and referring to the forthcoming Paris production of
Tannhäuser, Zurich, 19 September 1849
London £1,300 ($3,055). 30.IV.80

VLADIMIR ILYICH LENIN
An autograph letter testifying that Comrade
Henri Gilbeaux is a member of the French
Communist Party, Kremlin, Moscow,
3 May 1919
London £5,000 ($11,750). 29.IV.80

SIGMUND FREUD
An autograph letter to William Bayard Hale,
journalist and political commentator,
Vienna, 15 January 1922
New York $7,250 (£3,085). 9.IV.80

FRIEDRICH SCHILLER
The autograph manuscript of the revised final draft for his ballad
Der Graf von Hapsburg, 1803–1805
London £37,000 ($86,950). 30.IV.80

Fig 1

HERNANDO CORTES, MARQUES DEL VALLE DE OAXACA

A signed letter to Juan de Toledo, Sheriff of Teleauntepac, *circa* 1540–42

New York $20,000. 26.IV.78

Fig 2

SIR FRANCIS DRAKE

The signed deed of sale of Grayhurst Manor, given by Elizabeth I to Sir Francis in recognition of his voyage around the world, on vellum, 13 January 1582

New York $10,500. 20.VI.79

American historical documents

Jerry E. Patterson

American history dates from Independence, just over two hundred years ago, but the documentary record, beginning with the first exploration and settlement of the North American continent, covers a period more than twice that long. Very few collectors of American historical autographs and manuscripts have had the imagination, patience and means to attempt covering the four centuries of American history in their collections. One who successfully built such a collection was the late Philip D. Sang.

Philip Sang (1902–75), a Chicago businessman, formed his collection between 1950 and his death. From Hernando Cortes (Fig 1) to Lyndon B. Johnson, the important figures in American history were represented in autographic form. From the sixteenth century, were manuscripts of explorers and settlers, among them the rare autographs of Sir Francis Drake (Fig 2), Sir Walter Ralegh, Samuel de Champlain and Sir Ferdinando Gorges. The collection contained from the seventeenth century, autographs of all the important royal governors of the British colonies, leaders from the other colonies such as Director-General Peter Stuyvesant of New Amsterdam, lords proprietors such as the Penns, and Indian chiefs, including the celebrated Sachem, 'King Philip' (Fig 3). From the eighteenth century, military leaders of the colonial wars, governors, explorers, divines such as the Mather family and literary men were represented. In western Americana Mr Sang owned the rare autographs of Meriwether Lewis and William Clark, Daniel Boone, Christopher 'Kit' Carson and David Crockett. Every President of the United States from George Washington to Richard Nixon was represented in letters, documents and cheques. The Washington material (forty-four items) and the Lincoln material (over 100 items) was extensive and the collection was rich in presidential rarities, such as the signature of President William Henry Harrison, who held office for only one month (Fig 5).

The pivots of American autograph and manuscript collecting have always been the American Revolution and the Civil War, and the Sang Collection carried on the grand tradition with some of the most important material ever assembled on these major events. There were autograph letters of George Washington (Fig 4) and other Revolutionary generals, signers of the Declaration of Independence and the United States Constitution (complete sets), patriots and loyalists, spies, foreign soldiers who helped the American forces, among them the Marquis de Lafayette, Baron von Steuben, Count de Rochambeau and Tadeusz Kosciuszko. From the Civil War era were generals of both armies, including General Thomas J. 'Stonewall' Jackson, abolitionists such as John Brown of Osawatomie, and poets, among them Walt Whitman.

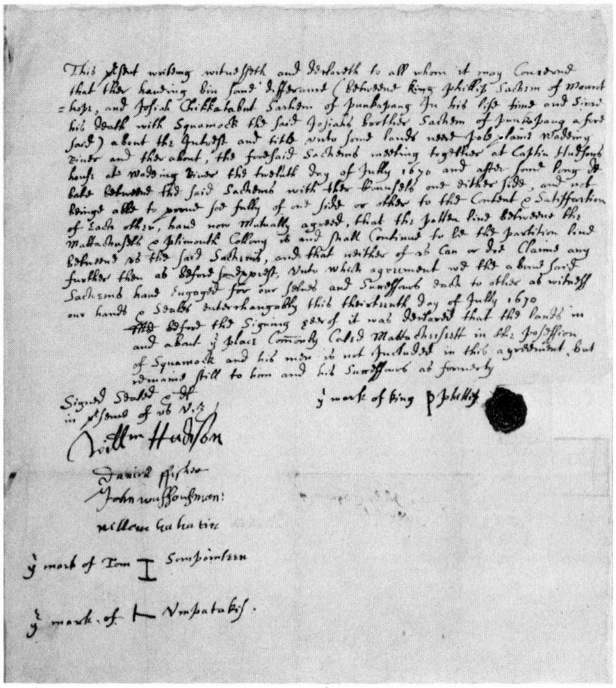

Fig 3
'KING PHILIP'
A manuscript treaty between the
American Indians and the Pilgrims,
signed with the Sachem's sign
manual, 13 July 1670
New York $8,000. 26.IV.78

Throughout the collection a special feel for quality and for the personal was striking. Among the military records of George Washington was a letter about finding a new cook and a plan for the house he hoped to build in the city named for him (Fig 9). Included with the Thomas Jefferson letters discussing the policies of the new Republic was one about his taste in wines. Amid the diplomatic correspondence, some of it in cipher, of Benjamin Franklin, America's ambassador to the Old World, was a trenchant letter complaining of the 'rogue' who had made a bad job of shoeing Franklin's horse. One of the more moving documents in the collection was the voucher for the final pay cheque that Jefferson Davis drew as President of the short-lived Confederate States of America.

Sophisticated autograph collecting explores subjects in depth. Mr Sang was fascinated, for example, by the best-known treason in American history, the offer made in 1780, by Major-General Benedict Arnold to the British spy Major John Andre to betray the American garrison at West Point. Andre was captured by the Americans and hanged. Arnold fled to Canada, then to England. The autographs relating to this treason included a journal of Major Andre, a letter from him notifying his superior, Sir Henry Clinton, of his capture, written just two days before his hanging, drawings of American subjects by Andre, who was a skilled amateur artist (Fig 7), the rare printed account of his trial and a letter in which Andre was notified of the hour of his execution (see *Art at Auction 1977–78*, p 185). In addition, Mr Sang owned the official edition (one of fifty copies) of an earlier court martial of Arnold, his memorandum book describing the Battle of Ticonderoga, his commission and his will. Important contemporary references to Arnold and Andre were found throughout: a letter from Samuel Huntington (Fig 6), signer of the Declaration of Independence,

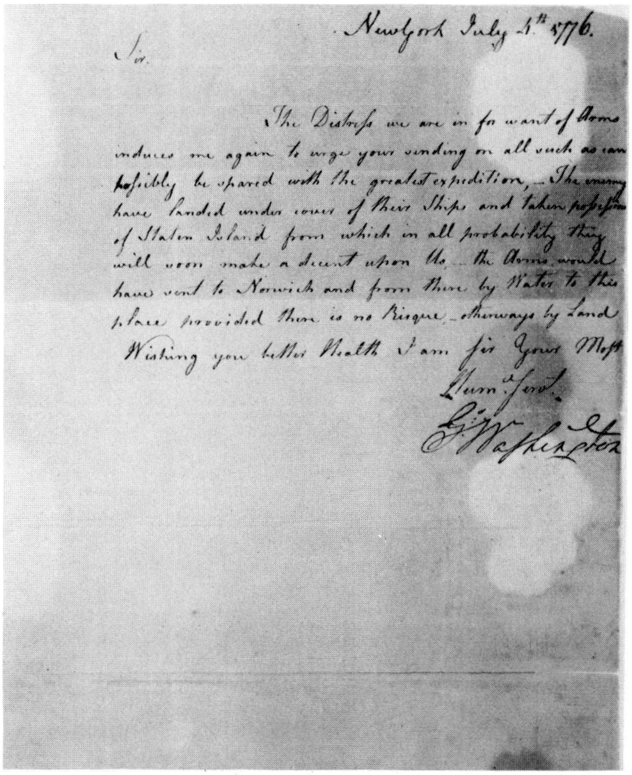
New York July 4th 1776.

Sir,

The Distress we are in for want of Arms induces me again to urge your sending on all such as can possibly be spared with the greatest expedition. The enemy have landed under cover of their Ships and taken possession of Staten Island from which in all probability they will soon make a decent upon us. The Arms would have sent to Norwich and from thence by Water to this place provided there is no Risque, otherways by Land. Wishing you better Health I am Sir Your Most Humd Servt.

Go Washington

Fig 4
GEORGE WASHINGTON
A signed letter to one of his generals requesting additional arms for the defence of New York, written before Washington had heard that Independence had been declared, 4 July 1776
New York $30,000 (£12,766). 3.VI.80

Fig 5 (*lower left*)
WILLIAM HENRY HARRISON
A signed letter to Benjamin Franklin Butler accepting his resignation as United States Attorney for the Southern District of New York, 5 March 1841
New York $28,000. 14.XI.78

Fig 6 (*below*)
SAMUEL HUNTINGTON
An autograph letter to General Nathanael Greene concerning the treason of Benedict Arnold, 27 September 1780
New York $5,250. 14.XI.78

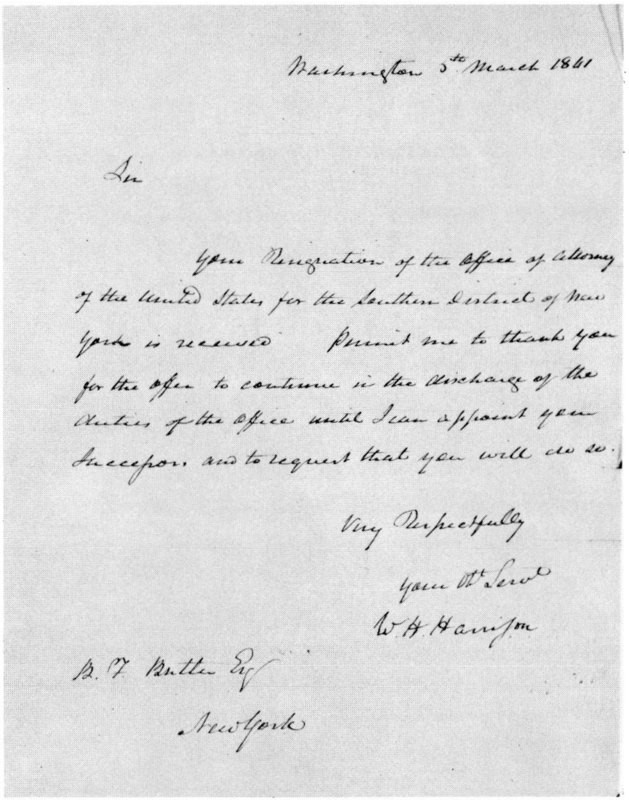
Washington 5th March 1841

Sir

Your Resignation of the Office of Attorney of the United States for the Southern District of New York is received. Permit me to thank you for the offer to continue in the discharge of the duties of the Office until I can appoint your Successor, and to request that you will do so.

Very Respectfully
Your Obt Servt
W H Harrison

B. F. Butler Esq
New York

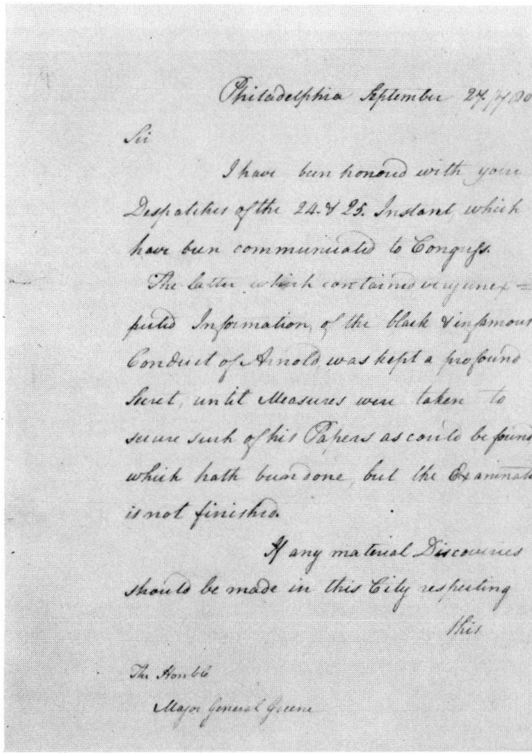
Philadelphia September 27, 1780

Sir

I have been honored with your Despatches of the 24 & 25 Instant which have been communicated to Congress.

The Letter which contained the unexpected Information of the black & infamous Conduct of Arnold was kept a profound Secret, until Measures were taken to secure such of his Papers as could be found which hath been done, but the Examination is not finished.

If any material Discoveries should be made in this City respecting this

The Honble
Major General Greene

Fig 7
MAJOR JOHN ANDRE
A pencil drawing of an American Indian dance with settlers and soldiers, 8½in by
15¾in (21.5cm by 40cm)
New York $3,500. 26.IV.78

referring to 'the black & infamous conduct of Arnold'; a letter from Richard Varick, who had been Arnold's *aide-de-camp*, was later Washington's secretary and, finally, Mayor of New York City, discussing the treason of his former superior officer; a letter from Captain Jonathan Ten Eyck calling the treachery 'a masterpiece of villany [*sic*]'; and one from Thomas Paine to General Nathanael Greene about Andre saying 'he died like a Roman'. In 1821, Major Andre was reburied in Westminster Abbey; a ceremony to which three letters in the Sang Collection referred.

Other sections of the collection were equally comprehensive. The Abraham Lincoln material included not only some of the finest autograph letters of the President and letters by his family, friends and official associates, but items such as an original poem, written by Lincoln as a young man in Illinois, describing a bear hunt. Subsidiary material included a manuscript of Walt Whitman's *O Captain! My Captain!*, his poem on Lincoln's death (Fig 8), and important manuscripts by Carl Sandburg, known as the poet of Chicago and Lincoln's biographer.

All great autograph collectors have their special affections and Mr Sang's was for cheques signed or endorsed by noted persons. Of great rarity were cheques by Presidents Rutherford B. Hayes, Herbert Hoover and John F. Kennedy signed in office, and cheques signed by people as diverse as John Wilkes Booth, assassin of President Lincoln, and Charles Thomson, Secretary of the Continental Congress.

Philip Sang was generous in making his material available to scholars for research, and to the public for viewing. During his ownership the collection was exhibited at twenty institutions. With over half the collection purchased at Parke-Bernet in the 1950s and '60s, the four sales between April 1978 and June 1980 marked the dispersal of the most important body of American historical autographs and manuscripts assembled by a private collector this century.

O Captain! My Captain!

O Captain! my Captain! our fearful trip is done,
The ship has weather'd every rack, the prize we sought is won,
The port is near, the bells I hear, the people all exulting,
While follow eyes the steady keel, the vessel grim and daring.
But O heart! heart! heart!
O the bleeding drops of red,
Where on the deck my Captain lies,
Fallen cold and dead.

O Captain! my Captain! rise up and hear the bells;
Rise up — for you the flag is flung — for you the bugle trills,
For you bouquets and ribbon'd wreaths — for you the shores a-crowding,
For you they call, the swaying mass, their eager faces turning;
Here Captain! dear father!
This arm beneath your head!
It is some dream that on the deck
You've fallen cold and dead.

My Captain does not answer, his lips are pale and still,
My father does not feel my arm, he has no pulse nor will,
The ship is anchor'd safe and sound, its voyage closed and done,
From fearful trip the victor ship comes in with object won;
Exult O shores, and ring O bells!
But I with mournful tread,
Walk the deck my Captain lies,
Fallen cold and dead.

Walt Whitman

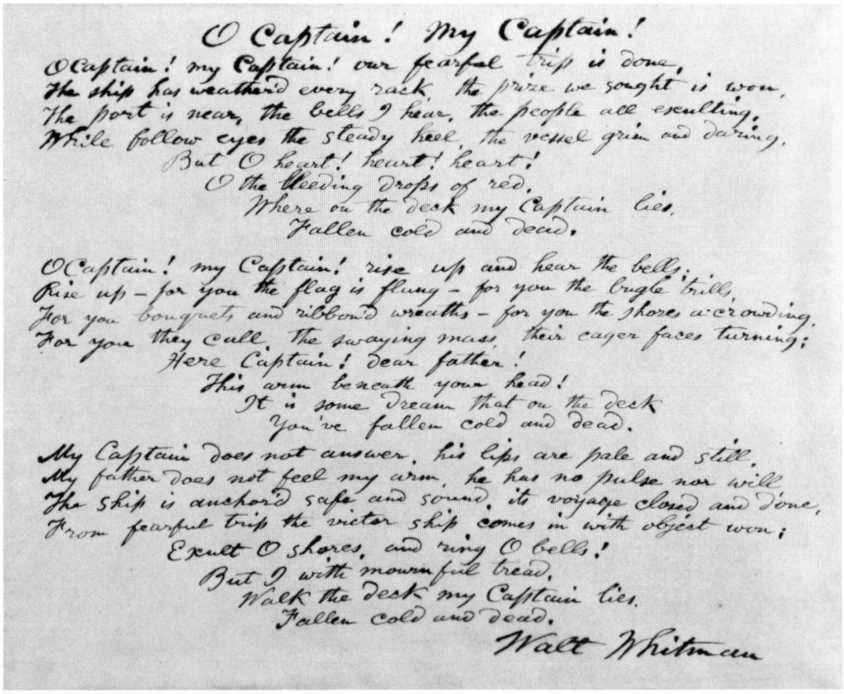

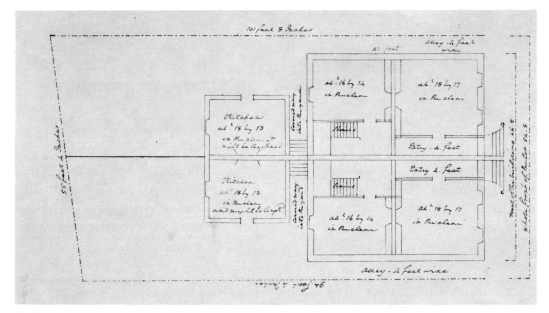

Fig 8
WALT WHITMAN
An autograph manuscript of *O Captain! My Captain!*, 1865
New York $15,000. 26.IV.78

Fig 9
GEORGE WASHINGTON
An autograph manuscript plan for a portion of his proposed adjoining houses in Washington DC, September 1798
New York $8,500. 26.IV.78

PAUL HOSTE
L'art des armées navales, first edition, Anisson & Posuel, Lyons, 1697
Milan L 1,600,000 (£815 : $1,914). 23.V.80

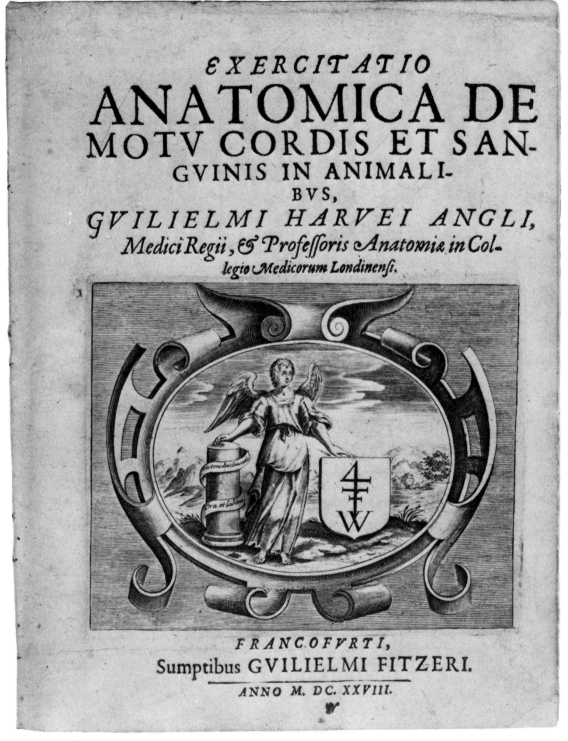

WILLIAM HARVEY
Exercitatio Anatomica de Motu Cordis et Sanguinis in Animalibus, first edition, William Fitzer,
Frankfurt, 1628
London £88,000 ($206,800). 6.XI.79
From the Honeyman Collection

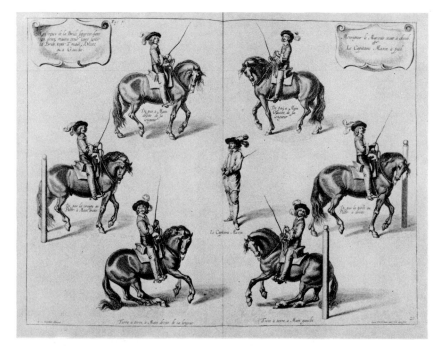

WILLIAM CAVENDISH, DUKE OF NEWCASTLE
A General System of Horsemanship in all its branches, two volumes,
J. Brindley, 1743
London £1,900 ($4,465). 1.X.79

JOHN JAMES AUDUBON
Birds of America, the original copper plate for the *Swallow-tailed Hawk*, engraved
by Robert Havell, London, 1829
New York $34,000 (£14,468). 27.XI.79

STRIX CANDIDA. *Tickell*

JOHN GOULD
The Birds of Asia, seven volumes, 530 hand-coloured lithographed plates by Gould, Richter
& Wolf, 1850–83
London £15,000 ($35,250). 9.VI.80

Voyage pittoresque par les lieux les plus interresans de la Suisse, fifty hand-coloured engraved plates,
Keller & Fussli, Zurich, *circa* 1827
New York $30,000 (£12,766). 27.XI.79

PIERRE LOUYS
Les Chansons de Bilitis, number six of twenty-five copies, with illustrations by
George Barbier, Pierre Bouchet, Paris, 1929
Monte Carlo FF 270,000 (£27,835:$65,412). 28.XI.79
From the collection of Claude Cartier

The whole ART of

LEGERDEMAIN:

OR,

Hocus Pocus

In PERFECTION.

By which the meaneſt Capacity may per-
form the Whole A R T without a
Teacher. Together with the Uſe of
all the Inſtruments belonging thereto. –

To which is now added,

Abundance of New and Rare Inventions,
the like never before in Print but much
deſired by many.

*The Fourth Edition, with large Additions and
Amendments.*

Written by H. D E A N.

L O N D O N:
Printed for *J. Hodges,* oppoſite St *Magnus* Church,
London Bridge; *C Hitch,* at the *Red-Lion* in
Pater-noster Row; and *R. Ware,* at the *Sun* and
Bible on *Ludgate-Hill.*

Strange Feats are herein taught by Slight of Hand,
With which you may divert yourſelf and Friend.
The like in Print was never ſeen before,
And ſo you'll ſay, when once you've read it o'er.

Fig 1
HENRY DEAN
The Whole Art of Legerdemain, or Hocus Pocus in Perfection, fourth edition, J. Hodges, C. Hitch and
R. Ware, *circa* 1758
Hodgson's Rooms £240. 5.VII.79

Hocus pocus

Raymond Toole Stott

Most collectors of conjuring books, like James B. Findlay, are themselves conjurers. They tend to be secretive, not only about how their tricks are performed but also about the books they collect, usually treatises on the art of conjuring. The sale and exchange of conjuring books has always been conducted either through booksellers or at the weekly meetings of magical societies, but rarely through public auction. Over the last fifty years it is doubtful whether more than twenty or thirty conjuring books have appeared at auction in England or America. In America the several important collections that have come up for sale on the death of their owners, were bought privately or by an institution. The Library of Congress acquired the Houdini Collection in this way.

The first conjuring collection sold in England was that of Roland Winder, at Sotheby's on 14 March 1974. A Yorkshireman and member of the Magic Circle, Winder owned some choice books such as Samuel Rid's *The Art of Jugling* (1612) and a first edition of the keystone of a conjuring collection – Reginald Scot's *Discoverie of Witchcraft* (1584). Winder was a stickler for condition, and most of the earlier books which had been published in boards or wrappers, were rebound in expensive calf, greatly appreciating the value. The original wrappers or boards were usually bound in at the end of the volume. Many of Findlay's books had been similarly rebound, mainly in cloth. Most of the items in the Winder Collection fetched high prices, but did not compare with those attained by Findlay's collection. A well-known and much sought-after periodical – *The Midget Magician* (1951–58) – limited to fifty copies and printed by a member of the conjuring community on an Adana press, the type having to be distributed after every four pages, fetched £55. Findlay's copy, bound in morocco but with the spines coming apart, went for £460($1,081).

James Black Findlay was born in Glasgow in 1905. He earned his first money on a newspaper round, and at fourteen-and-a-half left school and worked with his friend Duncan Johnston, delivering Keystone cop comedies to local cinemas. After seeing their first magic show they both decided to take up conjuring, bought a book on the subject – Hoffmann's *Modern Magic* – and began practising tricks. Soon they were good enough to take an engagement at a local lodge for a fee of 2s 6d. Later they performed a series of regular engagements with the Necessitous Children of Glasgow at 10s a time. With their earnings, Findlay and Johnston jointly built up a library. This they eventually divided when Johnston decided he wanted to concentrate solely on periodicals (he has the best collection in Europe today).

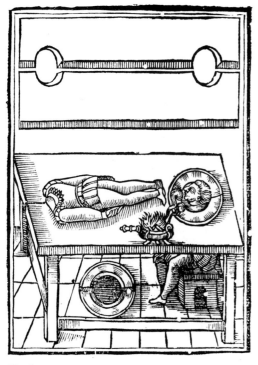

Fig 2
REGINALD SCOT
The Discovery of Witchcraft, third edition,
A. Clark & Dixy Page, 1665
Hodgson's Rooms £370 ($870). 4.X.79

Fig 3
Hocus Pocus Junior, the Anatomy of Legerdemain,
sixth edition, G. Dawson for Thomas Vere, 1663
Hodgson's Rooms £720. 5.VII.79

Findlay drifted into the furniture trade and after the Second World War left Glasgow to open a small hotel in Shanklin, in the Isle of Wight. Here he also set up as a bookseller. He used to boast that he never disposed of a book of which he had only one copy in his library. He continued to take engagements at parties and lectured in England, America and Canada. Gradually his collection grew to fill a large private room in the hotel. The spare spaces on the walls were occupied by posters and prints, and the top of the bookcases were lined with files containing letters from conjurers and fellow magic correspondents. One file was full of Houdini letters. The famous escapologist autographed so many books that it was said it was only the ones he had not signed that were worth collecting. Over the years Shanklin became the Mecca of conjurers from all parts of the world.

The art of conjuring, or juggling, as it used to be called, goes back to antiquity. Even while the priests of Egypt, Greece and Rome were using elaborate hydraulic, optical and aural illusions in the temples to awe the worshippers, charlatans were delighting street folk with tricks of sleight-of-hand and decapitation. One of the first to expose the use of magic by priests in the ancient temples was Hero of Alexander, a Greek mathematician and philosopher, probably of the latter half of the first century AD. He invented various contrivances such as Hero's Fountain, Penny in the Slot machines, a water organ and other apparatus employing steam. The first book, however, to expose the technique of conjuring was Reginald Scot's *The Discoverie of Witchcraft* (Fig 2), still in print after nearly 400 years and written to prove that demonstrations of legerdemain were not diabolical inventions, *ie* witchcraft, but a form of entertainment. King James VI of Scotland violently disagreed with this thesis and subsequently wrote his *Daemonologie* (1597) to support his argument.

In Scot's time the art of juggling was divided into three main categories, involving the use of balls, cards and money, and, as Scot emphasised, success in performance depended upon the extent of the deceit of spectators' eyes and judgements. The contemporary sleight-of-hand performer makes play with the same three items, and while technical skills have advanced prodigiously, some of the identical tricks are still popular today. One that was already old when Scot described it is the Cups and Balls (the old 'thimble-rig') (Fig 7), the mysterious transfer of a ball or pebble between three upturned cups. The conjurer performing this feat is depicted throughout history. According to E. A. Dawes, the earliest known illustration of the Cups and Balls is a coloured drawing of *The children of the planets*, 1404, by Joseph of Ulm, now in the University of Tubingen library, while the most famous representation is that of *The juggler* by Hieronymous Bosch, *circa* 1460–1516.

The Art of Jugling by Samuel Rid, the first work to be devoted exclusively to legerdemain, and *Hocus Pocus Junior* (1634), the first illustrated work on the subject, were both founded on Scot's work. In 1722, another book on conjuring based on Scot

Fig 4 (*left*)
The Whole Art of Legerdemain, or Hocus Pocus in Perfection, to which are added several Tricks of Cups and Balls, as performed by a Man without Hands or Feet, Bow Church Yard, *circa* 1755
Hodgson's Rooms £370 ($870). 4.X.79

Fig 5 (*below*)
Round about our Coal Fire, or Christmas Entertainments, fourth edition, J. Roberts, 1734
Hodgson's Rooms £520 ($1,222). 4.X.79

appeared, *The Whole Art of Legerdemain or Hocus Pocus in Perfection*, attributed to one Henry Dean. This was the first of a succession of editions (mostly unauthorised) published under this title with Dean's name on the title-page. Dean's identity is obscure. It is believed that he was a dealer in magical apparatus and had a bookstore in Tower Hill. In the fourth edition of *The Whole Art of Legerdemain* (Fig 1) an advertisement at the end of the volume reads: 'If any Person is desirous to be furnished with any of the instruments relating to this book . . . they may be furnished with the same at H. Dean's, near the Watch House on Little Tower Hill, Postern Row, a bookseller's Shop, the Open Bible being over the Door'.

The existence of these books and the tricks they contained gave rise to the 'juggler' or 'conjurer', who entertained passers-by in the street as he travelled from town to town and fair to fair, enlarging his repertoire as he went. Mattias Buchinger, who had neither hands nor feet, was referred to on the title-page of an anonymous edition of *The Whole Art of Legerdemain* (Fig 4). Some conjurers prospered like Isaac Fawkes, who left £10,000 when he died in 1731, and Christopher Pinchbeck, a clock and automaton maker, whose descendant, William Pinchbeck, was the author of the first original conjuring book to be published in the United States (Boston, 1805).

In the early nineteenth century, interest was more in mathematical precision and invention than in mystification and magical illusion. Competition became fierce. A man who thrived on it was John Henry Anderson, 'The Wizard of the North' (Fig 8). He compiled a brochure that sold at his show for one shilling which explained various tricks, and went on to expose the practices of 'Card Players, Blacklegs and Gamblers'. It was printed by job printers in the Seven Dials or the Cut, and went into 250 editions – at least, one appeared with that description on the title-page. Those from the Winder Collection fetched £20 each. Similar copies from Findlay's collection brought five times that amount. One of Anderson's competitors was Jean Eugène Robert-Houdin, an eminent clockmaker who was justly acclaimed as the father of modern magic.

The first time the word 'conjurer' was used to express a performer in sleight-of-hand was in Decremps' *The Conjurer Unmasked* (Fig 6), first published in 1785. Findlay had a copy of the 1788 edition. Other rare eighteenth- and nineteenth-century works included *Round about our Coal Fire* (Fig 5), which gave the first account of the folk-tale 'Jack and the Beanstalk', and Fairburn's *New London Conjuror*, with its fine hand-coloured frontispiece portraying conjuring scenes from old fairs (see *Art at Auction 1978–79*, p 198).

It is difficult to account for the stir aroused by the sale of the Findlay Collection and the dramatic impact it had on the conjuring world, particularly in America. Findlay had catholic taste. Nothing was ever spurned on grounds of condition. If he did not possess an item, he would buy it, even if it was imperfect, in the hope of finding a better copy later on. He owned an imperfect sixth edition of the rare *Hocus Pocus Junior* (Fig 3), of which only four copies of the first edition are known. It was soiled with ink scribbled in the margins and lacked the last nine leaves, but it was the only copy of the sixth edition ever traced. Findlay had acquired it from a fellow collector in the 1930s for £2. It went for £720 ($1,692). Many of his books were similarly imperfect, but the subject matter and range were astonishing.

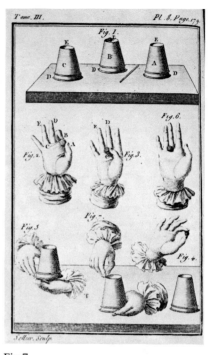

Fig 6
HENRI DECREMPS
The Conjurer Unmasked, second
edition 'with large additions and
alterations by T. Denton',
C. Stalker, 1788
Hodgson's Rooms £320. 5.VII.79

Fig 7
GILLES EDME GUYOT
*Nouvelles Récreations Physiques et
Mathématiques*, three volumes,
102 engraved plates, Paris, 1798
Hodgson's Rooms £105. 6.VII.79

The WIZARD OF THE NORTH exposing the trick " *Sauter la Coupe.*"

Fig 8
JOHN HENRY ANDERSON
*The Fashionable Science of Parlour
Magic, being the Newest Tricks of
Deception*, first edition, 'Temple of
Magic', 1843
Hodgson's Rooms £125. 5.VII.79

A Survey of London, by a Party of Tarry-at-Home Travellers, an engraved table game, hand-coloured and mounted on linen, W. Darton, 1820
Hodgson's Rooms £200 ($470). 6.VI.80

The Elopement, an engraved hand-coloured harlequinade, Robert Sayer, 1771
Hodgson's Rooms £360 ($846). 12.X.79

A Geographical Panorama, aquatint figures and views, forming nine scenes, Harvey, Darton & Co, 1822
Hodgson's Rooms £700 ($1,645). 6.VI.80

A Gift from the Gods to Mortals on Earth to Amuse and Mystify: Chung Ling Soo,
coloured lithograph, James Upton, Birmingham, *circa* 1905
Hodgson's Rooms £200 ($470). 3.VII.80

Jacobs' Farewell Night previous to his departure to Australia, a lithograph by
W. A. Smith, *circa* 1850
Hodgson's Rooms £680 ($1,598). 4.VII.80

The posters on this page were formerly in the collection of the late J. B. Findlay

TRISTAN TZARA
L'Antitête, three volumes, one of twenty-three
copies with extra suites of etched plates by
Joan Miró, Max Ernst and Yves Tanguy,
Bordas, Paris, 1949
Hodgson's Rooms £5,000 ($11,750). 16.XI.79
From the collection of Vera Ronnen-Wall

A. KRUCHENYKH and V. KHLEBNIKOV
Igra v adu (A Game in Hell), second
edition, Svet, St Petersburg, 1915
Hodgson's Rooms £1,150 ($2,703). 7.II.80

GEOFFREY CHAUCER
The Canterbury Tales, four volumes, one of fifteen copies
on vellum, wood-engravings by Eric Gill, Golden Cockerel
Press, Waltham St Lawrence, 1929–31
New York $27,500 (£11,702). 27.XI.79

ARTHUR RACKHAM
Common Objects at the Seaside by our Goblinesque Artist, an ink drawing, coloured and retitled *No. 2. Pleasure Seekers,* signed and dated *04*
Hodgson's Rooms £5,200 ($12,220). 26.X.79

SIDNEY PAGET
A wash drawing of Sherlock Holmes and Watson to illustrate *The Hound of the Baskervilles,* signed, *circa* 1902
Hodgson's Rooms £2,400 ($5,640). 25.VII.80
From the collection of the Rev. J.R. Paget

WALTER CRANE
Christmas in Clover, the autograph manuscript and three watercolour drawings, signed, for an unpublished masque
Hodgson's Rooms £940 ($2,209). 11.VII.80

The Brighton Grammar School Annual Entertainment at the Dome, containing eleven of the earliest published drawings by Aubrey Beardsley, Brighton, 1888
Hodgson's Rooms £330 ($776). 1.V.80

J.R.R. TOLKIEN
The Lord of the Rings, three volumes, signed or inscribed by the author, 1954–55
Hodgson's Rooms £2,300 ($5,405). 23.V.80
From the collection of Father Francis Groot

SACHEVERELL SITWELL
Conversation Pieces, first edition, inscribed and with a pen and ink drawing by Rex Whistler, Batsford, 1936
Hodgson's Rooms £330 ($776). 22.V.80

Postage Stamps

SEYCHELLES, 1867 cover from the Seychelles with Mauritius 4d rose
Johannesburg R 700 (£389:$914). 19.X.79

SWITZERLAND, BASEL, 1845 2½r carmine, black and blue on envelope
London £8,500 ($19,975). 13.XII.79

NEW GUINEA, 1914 GRI
5s on 5 mark carmine
and black
London £2,000 ($4,700).
27.III.80

NATAL, 1902–1903
£20 red and green
Johannesburg R 16,000
(£8,889:$20,889). 19.X.79

RHODESIA, 1910–13   7s 6d
carmine and light blue
Johannesburg R 1,000
(£556:$1,306). 19.X.79

UNITED STATES OF
AMERICA, 1869
15¢ brown and blue,
centre inverted
New York $32,000
(£13,617). 7.II.80

UNITED STATES OF
AMERICA, 1869
30¢ blue and carmine,
flags inverted
New York $62,500
(£26,596). 7.II.80

UNITED STATES OF AMERICA, 1901 2¢ Pan-American,
centre inverted, reconstructed block of four
New York $220,000 (£93,617). 29.IV.80

UNITED STATES OF AMERICA, 1901 4¢ Pan-American,
centre inverted, block of four
New York $150,000 (£63,830). 29.IV.80

NIGER COAST, 1893
10s on 5d in vermilion
£5,250 ($12,338)

GREAT BRITAIN, 1840 2d blue, plate 1
£25,000 ($58,750)

NORTHERN NIGERIA,
1904 £25 green and
carmine
£26,000 ($61,100)

NEW BRUNSWICK, 1851
1s reddish mauve
£21,000 ($49,350)

MALAYA, JOHORE,
1922–40
$500 blue and red
£14,000 ($32,900)

NOVA SCOTIA, 1851–57
1s purple
£9,500 ($22,325)

GREAT BRITAIN,
1867–83
watermark Anchor,
white paper, 10s
greenish grey
£27,000 ($63,450)

MAURITIUS, 1848
early impression,
2d blue
£27,000 ($63,450)

CEYLON, 1912–25
1,000r purple on red
£12,000 ($28,200)

The stamps on this page are from the 'Vaduz' Collection and were sold in London on 29 November 1979

FALKLAND ISLANDS, 1861–77 black frank on envelope to Tobago
London £5,500 ($12,925). 27.IX.79

UNITED STATES OF AMERICA, 1869 1¢ buff vertical pair and single tied to cover with a
Waterbury, Connecticut, 'running chicken' cancellation
New York $240,000 (£102,128). 30.X.79

Collectors' Sales

An ormolu musical automaton in the form of a magician, on a rosewood base, by Jacques-François Houdin, mid-nineteenth century, height 15¼in (38.5cm)
Belgravia £8,000 ($18,800). 6.VI.80

A cigarette lighter within an architectural case, probably
German, mid nineteenth century, height 18in (45.5cm)
Belgravia £900 ($2,115). 30.XI.79

A Swiss velograph typewriter, *circa* 1887,
width 12in (30.5cm)
Belgravia £1,100 ($2,585). 7.IX.79

A Carette 2½in gauge 'III' live steam spirit-fired 4–2–0 locomotive, *circa* 1902, length 22¾in (58cm) Belgravia £1,400 ($3,290). 16.V.80

A Marklin tinplate battleship, *Weissenburg, circa* 1905, length 34½in (87.5cm)
PB Eighty-four $21,000 (£8,936). 5.XII.79
From the collection of the late Mercedes Sonnenthal

A painted wood figure of a river goddess and a dolphin, probably Flemish, seventeenth century, length $22\frac{1}{2}$in (57cm)
Belgravia £1,900 ($4,465). 5.X.79

The Sheid Collection
of nautical antiques

Hilary Kay

Frederick-Christian Sheid, the late Chairman of the Belgian shipping line and ship-building company L'Armement de Deppe, began collecting works of art relating to his trade during the 1930s. Over the following three decades a nautical collection of great diversity was compiled, ranging from navigational instruments of the eighteenth century to a cheroot cutter of the early twentieth century.

The collection's attraction was its lack of sophistication. There were more than 500 objects varying greatly in age, quality and value, which caught the interest of people who had perhaps previously regarded the collecting of maritime antiques as un-specialised and expensive. This was also the first time that such a diverse group had been sold together as an entity, appealing to collectors of books, maps, arms, armour, scientific instruments, precious metals, decorative art and ceramics.

The more unusual items in the collection were a Norwegian silver snuff box with a relief decoration on the lid of a frigate under full sail against a distant shore, inscribed *Amideste af Fregat Jkibet Elisabeth* and dated *1781*, and a pair of scrimshaw whale's teeth delicately inscribed with three-masted sailing vessels and long-boats pursuing whales. A fisherman's bone and silver 'Jonah and the Whale' knife and scabbard may have been sailor-work, silver mounted in port at a later date; this bore the name *Iasper De Rvddere* along one side and was dated *1643*. Sheid amassed over eighty model ships, of which several were made to scale for dockyards. These, together with earlier models of merchantmen and naval vessels were sharply contrasted by the naive simplicity of ships in bottles.

The more specialised nautical books, maps, atlases, pictures and prints, which related mainly to Antwerp and her environs and contained work by local artists and publishers, were of interest to Belgian or Dutch collectors. However, of international attraction were the figureheads and ships' fittings, which included small carvings of outstanding quality besides the larger prow decorations, and varied in date between the seventeenth and late nineteenth centuries (see opposite). Of particular appeal were the nautical and navigational instruments (octants, quadrants, sextants, equinoctial dials, compasses and timepieces) such as an Arnold & Dent eight-day marine chronometer no 646 and a commemorative clock inset into a casing in the form of a life-belt inscribed *Adolf Deppe*, the founder of L'Armement de Deppe.

The Sheid Collection was a personal achievement which attracted wide attention. Since many of the pieces had not previously appeared on the open market and because they were sold as an entity, a new enthusiasm was generated, encouraging collectors of all financial capabilities to explore the field of nautical antiques.

A pair of black enamel opera glasses with gilt-metal frame
and composition eye pieces and a beaver skin stovepipe
hat, extended length of glasses 3¾in (9.5cm); height of hat
8in (20cm)
New York, glasses $24,000 (£10,213); hat $10,000 (£4,255).
28.XI.79
From the collection of the late Roy P. Crocker

The hat was the property of Abraham Lincoln and the
glasses are said to have been picked up from the floor of
the President's box at Ford's Theatre after he had been
assassinated on 14 April 1865

An American Mills 'Dewey' 5¢ one-wheel slot machine,
circa 1900, height 66in (167.5cm)
PB Eighty-four $9,000 (£3,830). 5.III.80

Above A painted wood 'Dapper Dan' shop figure,
Philadelphia or Washington DC, *circa* 1880,
height 76in (193cm)
$49,000 (£20,851)

Right A painted wood figure of a race track tout on a
pedestal base by Charles Dowler, Providence,
Rhode Island, *circa* 1895, height 79in (200.5cm)
$53,000 (£22,553)

The figures on this page are from the collection of Mr
and Mrs Francis Andrews and were sold in New York
on 1 May 1980

A painted wood American eagle wall plaque, attributed to John Bellamy, *circa* 1860,
length 39in (99cm)
Pokety Farms $39,000 (£16,596). 24.V.80
From the collection of the late Bernice Chrysler Garbisch

Works of Art

A bronze medallion of a winged victory, from a set of six by Jean Arnould after designs by Pierre Mignard for La Place des Victoires, Paris, *circa* 1685, diameter 29$\frac{7}{8}$in (76cm)
Monte Carlo FF1,200,000 (£123,711 : $290,722). 27.V.80
From the collection of the Conyngham Heirlooms Trust

A Limoges enamel reliquary *châsse* of Thomas à Becket, *circa* 1195, height $11\frac{3}{4}$in (30cm)
London £420,000 ($987,000). 13.XII.79
From the collection of Ernst and Marthe Kofler-Truniger

A reliquary *châsse* of Thomas à Becket

Simone Caudron

The reliquary *châsse* of Thomas à Becket, from the collection of M. et Mme Kofler-Truniger (see opposite), is one of the most significant landmarks of Limoges medieval enamelling, not only because of its workmanship, but also on account of its provenance and its history. Its large size, elongated proportions, decorative detail and transparently Romanesque figure style date it at around 1195.

The *châsse* has been in England since the middle ages. To escape the grasp of the iconoclasts during the Reformation, it was hidden by a papist family in St Neots, near Peterborough, re-emerging in the mid eighteenth century when it passed into the hands of the antiquarian William Stukeley. It was the medieval quality and the unusual decoration of the shrine which caught Stukeley's eye; connoisseurs of the period were not familiar with Limoges works of art, the origins of which had been lost for centuries. Stukeley suggested in a speech to the Royal Society in 1748 that the *châsse* was of Saxon origin, concluding that the martyrdom depicted was that of Abbot Theodore of Croyland who was murdered at the altar by the Danes in 870. Not until the 1930s (by which time the Limoges craftsmanship was no longer in question) was Tancred Borenius able to confirm, on the basis of a strict iconographical analysis, that the martyr represented on the Kofler *châsse* was indeed Thomas à Becket.

Up to now, forty-five Limoges *châsses* depicting the murder of Becket and similar in composition have been recorded. Of the clerics who suffered martyrdom at the altar, Thomas à Becket was the only one whose remains were conserved and dispersed throughout Christendom. This was done to secure the importance of Canterbury as the seat of Christianity in England, and to ensure the financial support necessary for enriching the Cathedral. The Kofler *châsse* must be considered first in this series of shrines: its size is unusual and it displays an exceptional number of scenes and figures. Moreover, the placement of the figure of Christ on one of the gable ends together with the four saints flanking the diaper-patterned panels on the back, is a curious arrangement. In no other Limoges *châsse* is the certainty of ecclesiastical authority and holiness asserted with such strength. This dogmatic pictorial layout suggests that the piece was specially commissioned. It is plausible that Benedict, Abbot of Peterborough, could have ordered the shrine from a Limoges workshop before his own death in 1194. (He was a friend of Richard I, himself patron of the Limoges enamellers for Grandmont Priory.) Benedict had previously been chancellor to the Archbishop of Canterbury, and had brought Becket's relics to Peterborough in 1177, when he was appointed head of the Abbey.

A Byzantine ivory relief of the Hodegetria, late tenth century, height 6in (15cm)
London £35,000 ($82,250). 13.XII.79
From the collection of Ernst and Marthe Kofler-Truniger

A Burgundian Romanesque limewood Crucifix figure, second quarter twelfth century,
height 43½in (110.5cm)
London £210,000 ($493,500). 13.XII.79
Formerly in the collection of the late Adolphe Stoclet

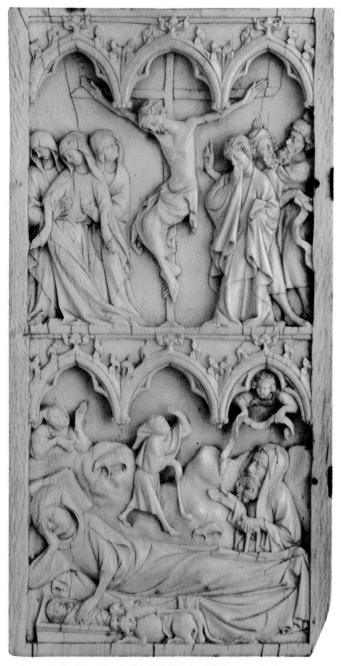

A French Gothic ivory relief of the Crucifixion and the
Nativity, late fourteenth century, height 7⅛in (18cm)
New York $27,000 (£11,489). 8.XII.79
From the collection of Mr and Mrs J. L. Lewin

A French Gothic ivory group of the Virgin and Child, first half fourteenth century,
height 7¾in (19.5cm)
London £22,000 ($51,700). 13.XII.79
From the collection of Ernst and Marthe Kofler-Truniger

A South German pearwood figure of an old woman, *circa* 1525, height $5\frac{7}{8}$in (15cm)
London £21,000 ($49,350). 13.XII.79

From left to right
A Swabian or Upper Rhine
limewood figure of St Verena,
late fifteenth century,
height 27¼in (69cm)
A Swabian or Upper Rhine
limewood figure of St Barbara,
late fifteenth century,
height 28½in (72.5cm)
A Swabian or Upper Rhine
limewood figure of
St Catherine, late fifteenth
century, height 28¾in (73cm)

These figures were sold as one
lot in London on 13 December
1979 for £58,000 ($136,300)

A Franconian limewood relief of the
Annunciation, from the workshop
of Tilman Riemenschneider,
circa 1500–1510, height 22¾in (58cm)
London £24,000 ($56,400). 13.XII.79

Fig 1
An amber chess set and board, probably
German, eighteenth century, height of pieces
1¾in to 2¾in (4.5cm to 7cm)
New York $23,000 (£9,787). 5.X.79
From the Harbeson Collection

Fig 2
A German wood and ceramic games board inlaid
with fruitwood, early seventeenth century,
diameter 14½in (37cm)
New York $36,000 (£15,319). 5.X.79
From the Harbeson Collection

Fig 3
A tortoise-shell-veneered board inlaid with
mother-of-pearl, copper and stained ivory
from a board and chess set, Augsburg, early
eighteenth century, diameter 19⅛in (48.5cm)
Belgravia £15,500 ($36,425). 15.IV.80

Chess sets and the Harbeson Collection

David Hafler

Chess is a game – a war game between opposing armies in which the pieces represent various military ranks from generals (kings) down to foot soldiers (pawns). From the earliest days of chess, about 1,400 years ago, chess pieces have been either representational, indicative of the function of the piece, or abstract and symbolic. Because chess was a game, not an art form, most of the pieces were generally utilitarian, with little intrinsic value. Through breakage and loss the early sets were decimated, and there are no known complete sets from the first 900 years of chess history. Only a few isolated pieces have survived those early years, and these are valued for their rarity and historical interest rather than their beauty. In more recent years, chess sets which have been made primarily for play are still utilitarian and have little value as art objects. However, not all sets have been made for play; and just as skilled artisans have turned other utilitarian objects into artifacts of beauty, they did this also with chess, which came to achieve a dual role – as a game and as an ornament for display. This concept of chess as a showpiece became important in the seventeenth and eighteenth centuries, and continues today.

Chess sets have been made in a wide variety of materials, in addition to the wood and ivory which are used in most sets for play. Less common materials include amber (Fig 1), precious metals, jade, tortoise-shell (Fig 3), coral and mother-of-pearl. The themes and figures illustrated in chess sets are wide-ranging; from battles to fish (Fig 4) or insects. There are also sets of abstract sculpture and whimsical sets.

Modern artists, Man Ray, Max Ernst and Salvador Dali, have made and signed chess sets, but older chess sets are rarely identified as to maker. The historical background or provenance of antique sets is rarely known, with the exception of marked sets of silver or porcelain. This is one of the difficulties of buying chess sets; the purchaser must be knowledgeable or must buy from a knowledgeable source. The channels of distribution are very limited due to the small number of sets which are available and the few specialists in this field. Sales are infrequent, and therefore, it was a significant event for chess enthusiasts when the Harbeson Collection of chess items was sold in New York on 6 October 1979.

John F. Harbeson, a prominent Philadelphia architect and former Professor of Architecture at the University of Pennsylvania, collected chess sets and related items for more than fifty years. He started his collection unexpectedly and with no intent to build one of the world's most extensive and beautiful collections. Harbeson was travelling in Ireland in 1927, a period of Black and Tan political problems, when many

Fig 4
An Italian ivory chess set, mid–late eighteenth century, height of pieces $2\frac{1}{4}$in to $4\frac{1}{4}$in (5.7cm to 10.8cm) New York $10,000(£4,255). 6.II.80

British residents were moving back to England. Possessions were sold to simplify moving, and second-hand and antique shops were filled with discarded property. Harbeson noticed seven interesting chess sets in one shop which immediately attracted his interest, and that was the start of his collection. From then on, he sought chess sets wherever he could. He studied chess and its history carefully and became an authority. He wrote a chapter on chess in art and archaeology for the first book devoted to the subject, *Chessmen* (1937) by Donald Liddell.

The Harbeson Collection was eclectic, representing countries around the world and covering more than half the historical span of chess. Harbeson's aim was to acquire variety in chess forms and materials with no attempt at specialisation. When he was unable to find sets to add to his collection, he started to design and fabricate his own. Of special interest in the collection were the wide assortment of chess boards (Figs 1 and 2), and a Bohemian set carved in pearwood with all major pieces mounted on horseback or donkey. With such plebian material as wood, the unknown carver produced a set of great beauty and delicacy. John Harbeson was always happy to show his sets and share his knowledge. His home became a meeting place for chess collectors, attracting visitors from around the world. He willingly lent sets for exhibitions, the most important of which was Nine Centuries of Chessmen, a show of 346 exhibits held at the Philadelphia Museum of Art in 1964. His collection reached a level of about 400 chess items, comprising sets of thirty-two chessmen, groups of figures from incomplete sets and single boards. Part of the collection was dispersed by gifts to museums, libraries, his family and friends. At the age of ninety-one, John Harbeson decided to sell the balance of his collection: the largest and most important selection of chess items to be offered in the last twenty-five years.

From left to right
A Carolingian bronze key, ninth century, length $5\frac{1}{8}$in (13cm)
SFr9,500 (£2,436 : $5,724)
A French steel key, seventeenth century, length $5\frac{7}{8}$in (15cm)
SFr2,600 (£667 : $1,567)
A French steel key, seventeenth century, length $4\frac{5}{8}$in (11.7cm)
SFr1,400 (£359 : $844)
A German steel key, early eighteenth century, length $6\frac{1}{2}$in (16.5cm)
SFr1,400 (£359 : $844)

The keys on this page were sold in Zurich on 7 May 1980

A French ivory group of the martyrdom of St Bartholomew attributed to Jacques Lagneau,
first half seventeenth century, height 20in (51cm)
London £15,000 ($35,250). 17.IV.80

A bronze bust of Ottavio Farnese by Piero Paolo Romano, called Galeotti, signed, *circa* 1550–60, height 34½in (87.5cm)
Monte Carlo FF 950,000 (£97,938 : $230,155). 27.V.80

A Paduan bronze oil lamp in the form of a monster, sixteenth century, length 6in (15.2cm)
£15,500 ($36,425)

A Paduan bronze group of a lizard and a frog, from the workshop of
Andrea Briosco, called Riccio, early sixteenth century,
length 3⅛in (8cm)
£5,000 ($11,750)

A Paduan bronze group of two toads, early sixteenth century,
length 5in (12.7cm)
£6,000 ($14,100)

The bronzes on these pages were sold in London on 17 July 1980

A bronze figure of a naked youth representing Comedy and Tragedy by
Sir Alfred Gilbert, *circa* 1892, height 14⅜in (36.5cm)
Belgravia £6,600 ($15,510). 26.III.80
From the collection of Miss P. Kraay

A bronze group of two steeplechasers by Isadore Bonheur, signed and inscribed,
circa 1860, height 36in (91.5cm)
Belgravia £8,500 ($19,975). 26.III.80

A double-sided processional icon, the reverse showing St Nicholas, dated *7040* (1531 AD),
Novgorod, 19⅛in by 15in (48.5cm by 38cm)
London £25,000 ($58,750). 3.XII.79

A Byzantine icon of the martyr St Paraskevi, *circa* 1300,
4¾in by 3¾in (12cm by 9.5cm)
London £3,600 ($8,460). 2.VI.80

A Fabergé silver-gilt and shaded enamel liqueur set, workmaster Fedor Rückert,
Moscow, *circa* 1902, height of carafe 12⅜in (31.5cm)
New York $39,000(£16,596). 11.XII.79
From the collection of Mrs Boris Chaliapin

A Fabergé silver-mounted mahogany table, workmaster Julius Rappoport, Moscow, *circa* 1900,
height 2ft 4⅜in (72cm)
New York $22,000 (£9,362). 24.VI.80

A Fabergé agate owl, workmaster Henrik Wigström, St Petersburg, *circa* 1900, height 5in (12.5cm)
New York $85,000 (£36,170). 24.VI.80
From the collection of M. T. Heller II

A Fabergé nephrite hippopotamus fitted as a cigar lighter, St Petersburg, *circa* 1908,
length 7¾in (19.5cm)
New York $55,000 (£23,404). 11.XII.79
From the collection of Raymond Schlager

A Fabergé two-colour gold, enamel and diamond Imperial presentation snuff box inset with a
miniature of Nicholas II by A. Blaznov, signed, workmaster Mikhail Perchin, St Petersburg,
late nineteenth century, width 3⅛in (8cm)
Zurich SFr 175,000 (£44,872: $105,449). 14.XI.79
From the collection of the late Carel Repelaer

A Fabergé two-colour gold and enamel *nécessaire*, workmaster Henrik Wigström, St Petersburg,
circa 1912, width 4⅜in (11cm)
Zurich SFr 85,000 (£21,795: $51,218). 14.XI.79

A gold and hardstone snuff box, the rim engraved *Neuber à Dresde, circa* 1780, the agate cameo carved by Angelo Amastini, width 2¾in (7cm)
Zurich SFr 180,000 (£46,154:$108,462). 14.XI.79

A gold-mounted piqué snuff box, maker's mark of Pierre-François Drais, Paris, 1767,
width 2¼in (5.7cm)
Zurich SFr 52,000 (£13,333:$31,333). 14.XI.79

A Louis XV gold and enamel snuff box, maker's mark of Michel-Robert Hallé, Paris, 1749, width 2¾in (7cm)
New York $77,000 (£32,766). 24.X.79

An English enamel plaque painted with a portrait of
Queen Charlotte, wife of George III, *circa* 1761,
height 4⅛in (10.5cm)
London £3,600 ($8,460). 17.VI.80
Formerly in the collection of the late the
Hon. Mrs Nellie Ionides

An English enamel snuff box, *circa* 1760, width 3⅝in
(9.2cm)
New York $4,250 (£1,809). 17.V.80
From the collection of the late Bernice Chrysler Garbisch

An English enamel casket containing two caddies and a canister, *circa* 1760–65, width $8\frac{1}{4}$in (21cm)
London £4,200 ($9,870). 17.VI.80
Formerly in the collection of the late the Hon. Mrs Nellie Ionides

A gold snuff box, the rim engraved *Gouers AParis*, 1733, width 2¾in (7cm)
London £22,000 ($51,700). 3.VII.80

A gold presentation snuff box, maker's mark of A. J. Strachan, London, 1818, width 4⅜in (11cm)
London £27,000 ($63,450). 24.III.80
From the collection of the late Barbara Woolworth Hutton

A four-colour gold snuff box, the central medallion chased by George Michael Moser, maker's mark of Paul Bocquet, London, 1774, width 2⅝in (6.8cm)
London £27,000 ($63,450). 24.III.80
From the collection of the late
Barbara Woolworth Hutton

A gold presentation table snuff box, maker's mark IC, London, 1765, width 4in (10.2cm)
London £42,500 ($99,875). 24.III.80
From the collection of the late Barbara Woolworth Hutton

A four-colour gold and enamel singing bird box, maker's
mark CI, Geneva, *circa* 1820, width 3in (7.7cm)
Zurich SFr 40,000 (£10,256:$24,103). 14.XI.79

A gold and black onyx repeating clock by Cartier,
circa 1925, height 4¼in (10.7cm)
Zurich SFr 43,000 (£11,026:$25,910). 14.XI.79

A *boîte à portrait* and watch, the miniature by
Jean-Baptiste Isabey, signed, maker's mark
JAG, Paris, *circa* 1800–1810,
length 3⅜in (8.6cm)
Zurich SFr 50,000 (£12,821:$30,128). 6.V.80

MADEMOISELLE HENRIETTE JÜGEL
A young man seated in a prison cell, signed on the mount, dated *Berlin den I'' Januar 1807*,
$5\frac{1}{4}$in (13.5cm)
Zurich SFr 18,000 (£4,615:$10,846). 13.XI.79

RICHARD CROSSE, after REYNOLDS
Maria Waldegrave, Duchess of Gloucester, seated with her son, William
Frederick, later 2nd Duke of Gloucester and Edinburgh, 1779,
6⅝in (17cm)
London £7,800 ($18,330). 30.VI.80

This miniature is after the portrait of the Duchess at Buckingham Palace,
but has the addition of the child and dog and an altered background

NATHANIEL PLIMER
A young lady, *circa* 1790,
$2\frac{5}{8}$in (6.8cm)
London £3,500 ($8,225). 30.VI.80

RICHARD COSWAY
A young man, signed and dated
1790 on the reverse, $2\frac{7}{8}$in (7.4cm)
London £4,200 ($9,870). 30.VI.80

JOHN SMART
Dr James Anderson of the
East India Company,
signed and dated *1800*,
$2\frac{3}{4}$in (6.9cm)
London £7,000 ($16,450).
24.III.80

CHARLES SHIRREFF
An officer of the Royal
Artillery, *circa* 1790,
2in (5cm)
London £1,600 ($3,760).
30.VI.80

SAMUEL SHELLEY
Marlborough Parsons Sterling of
the 36th Foot, *circa* 1785,
$2\frac{1}{2}$in (6.4cm)
London £1,600 ($3,760). 30.VI.80

NICHOLAS HILLIARD
Jane Boughton, on vellum, inscribed and dated *1574*, 1⅝in (4.2cm)
London £75,000 ($176,250). 24.III.80
From the collection of the late A. C. Ward-Boughton-Leigh

An Elizabethan portrait

Roy Strong

The art of Nicholas Hilliard erupts so suddenly upon the Elizabethan world that it only serves to emphasise his genius. With an abruptness that is startling there begins, in 1572, that procession of likenesses which 400 years later still continue to astound us as the most complete expression of the Elizabethan aesthetic. Early miniatures are rare and only a handful survive from the period between 1572 and 1576, when Hilliard left for France. Most, too, are faded, damaged or retouched.

Jane Boughton (see opposite) is exceptional in the first place for its pristine condition. In this miniature we savour to the full the vigour of the artist's brushwork which, under intense magnification, has a cut and thrust as it twirls and whirls its way across the minute surface, suggesting the bristle of a starched lace ruff, the wiriness of crimped auburn hair, and the glitter of gold catching the light, whether on her caul, the looped chains across her bodice or in the embroidery on her lace partlet. And yet the key to a great Hilliard miniature is the artist's engagement with the sitter. Even in tired old age, Hilliard bestirred himself if a pretty girl enchanted him. Here he was clearly fascinated by this bold young woman with her bewitching brown eyes. In his own words this is what moved him to 'watch these lovely graces, witty smilings, and these stolen glances which suddenly like lightning pass, and another countenance taketh place'.

In 1574, when the miniature was painted, Jane Coningsby was twenty-one and had been married for at least three years (a son, Edward, had been born in 1572). Her husband was William Boughton of Little Lawford, Warwickshire, later to be twice sheriff of the county. Although Hilliard was already painting the Queen, his sitters during these years were not necessarily aristocratic. He had only just finished his seven-year apprenticeship under the Queen's jeweller, Robert Brandon. His work as a goldsmith still remains to be disentangled, if ever it can be, but portrait miniatures may well have begun as a kind of side line. What never ceases to amaze is his emergence at twenty-five as a mature artist. None of these miniatures from the early 1570s are in the least weak or tentative. His control of the placing of the figure within the picture's surface is total, as is his handling of his medium.

The portrait of Jane Boughton provides abundant evidence that, contrary to what has been written, Hilliard left for France in the autumn of 1576 as a fully developed artist confirming the poet Ronsard's withering comment on the English, that 'the islands indeed seldom bring forth any cunning man, but when they do it is in high perfection'.

JEREMIAH MEYER, after REYNOLDS
John Manners, Marquess of
Granby, enamel, signed and dated
1770, 4in (10.2cm)
London £8,000 ($18,800).
10.XII.79

CORNELIUS JOHNSON
A gentleman, on copper,
circa 1620, 2⅛in (5.4cm)
London £3,500 ($8,225). 1.V.80
From the Holzscheiter Collection

ISAAC OLIVER
A young lady, on vellum,
circa 1615, 2in (5cm)
London £13,000 ($30,550).
10.XII.79

RICHARD GIBSON
A young lady, possibly Elizabeth
Capel, Countess of Carnarvon,
on card, *circa* 1650, 2⅜in (6cm)
London £4,200 ($9,870). 30.VI.80

Jewellery

An emerald and diamond diadem, the emerald drops with individual eighteenth-century mounts
weighing approximately 605 carats
Zurich SFr 2,700,000 (£692,308:$1,626,923). 15.XI.79

According to family tradition, the emeralds formed part of the French Imperial Crown Jewels

A topaz and diamond demi-parure comprising a pendant, a pair of pendent earrings and a brooch,
circa 1800
London £6,500 ($15,275). 22.V.79

An emerald and diamond demi-parure comprising a pendant and a pair of pendent earrings, *circa* 1860
London £120,000 ($282,000). 27.IX.79

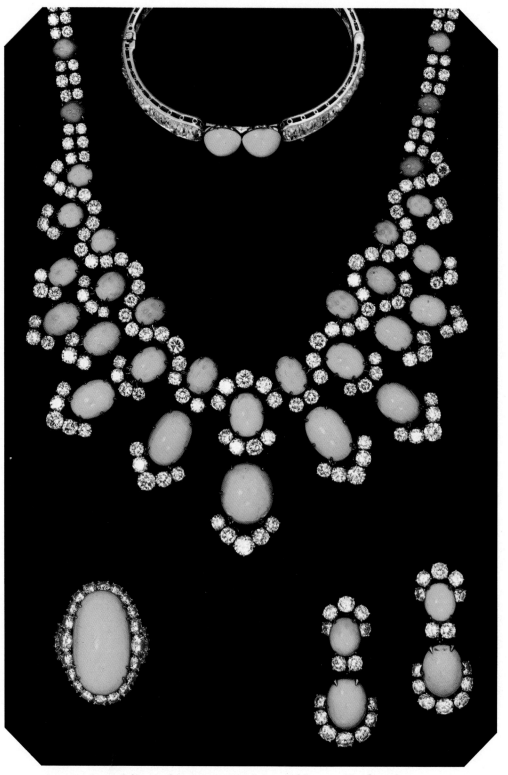

A turquoise and diamond parure comprising a necklace, a pair of pendent
earrings, a bangle and a ring
Zurich SFr 92,000 (£23,590:$55,436). 14.XI.79

A platinum and emerald-cut diamond necklace, the diamonds weighing
approximately 83 carats
New York $650,000 (£276,596). 24.IV.80

A pair of diamond pendent earrings, the circular-cut diamonds weighing 21.04 carats and 20.73 carats respectively
London £190,000 ($446,500). 27.IX.79
From the collection of HRH Prince Tomislav of Yugoslavia

A marquise-shaped diamond ring, the diamond weighing 21.54 carats, by Harry Winston
St Moritz SFr 2,000,000 (£512,821:$1,205,128). 16.II.80

A sapphire and diamond pendant, the central cabochon sapphire weighing approximately 15.4 carats
New York $240,000 (£102,128). 17.X.79

A step-cut sapphire ring, the sapphire weighing approximately 66.03 carats
Zurich SFr 2,300,000 (£589,744:$1,385,897). 8.V.80

A platinum, ruby and diamond bracelet, the central emerald-cut and the half moon-shaped diamonds weighing approximately 27.9 carats, and the square-cut rubies weighing approximately 22 carats
Los Angeles $150,000 (£63,830). 10.III.80
From the collection of the late Carma Israel

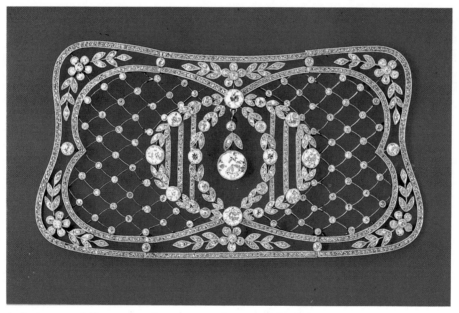

A platinum and diamond neck ornament, the central diamond weighing approximately 2.25 carats, *circa* 1900
PB Eighty-four $14,000 (£5,957). 27.III.80

A ruby and diamond corsage ornament, *circa* 1880
London £175,000 ($411,250). 27.IX.79

An emerald, ruby and diamond necklace by Cartier
New York $195,000 (£82,979). 6.XII.79
From the collection of the late Mabel Brady Garvan

1   A star ruby (approx 11 carats) ring, Hong Kong HK$200,000 (£17,391:$40,870). 23.V.80
2   A cabochon sapphire (approx 17.35 carats) and diamond ring, *circa* 1920, New York $205,000 (£87,234). 24.IV.80
3   A cushion-shaped ruby (3.32 carats) and diamond ring, Zurich SFr 180,000 (£46,154:$108,462). 7.V.80
4   A marquise-shaped diamond (approx 6.75 carats) ring, New York $290,000 (£123,404). 17.X.79
5   A cabochon emerald (approx 3.5 carats) and diamond ring, Hong Kong HK$170,000 (£14,783:$34,739). 23.V.80
6   An emerald-cut alexandrite (12.12 carats), New York $95,000 (£40,426). 24.IV.80
7   A cushion-shaped fancy green-yellow diamond (3.01 carats) ring, Zurich SFr 90,000 (£23,077:$54,231). 8.V.80
8   A ruby (approx 17 carats) and diamond ring, New York $500,000 (£212,766). 24.IV.80
9   A black opal and diamond ring, Zurich SFr 30,000 (£7,692:$18,077). 15.XI.79
10 A jade and diamond ring, Hong Kong HK$105,000 (£9,130:$21,457). 3.XII.79
11 An emerald-cut diamond (approx 22.3 carats) ring, New York $975,000 (£414,894). 17.X.79
12 A cat's eye (16.77 carats) and diamond ring, Hong Kong HK$250,000 (£21,739:$51,087). 3.XII.79
13 A cushion-shaped sapphire (approx 6.5 carats) and diamond ring, New York $80,000 (£34,043). 24.IV.80
14 A star sapphire (41.17 carats) and diamond ring, Hong Kong HK$140,000 (£12,174:$28,609). 23.V.80
15 A step-cut fancy yellow diamond (3.98 carats) ring, Zurich SFr 58,000 (£14,872:$34,949). 8.V.80
16 An emerald-cut fancy blue diamond (3.59 carats), New York $165,000 (£70,213). 24.IV.80
    From the collection of the late Bernice Chrysler Garbisch

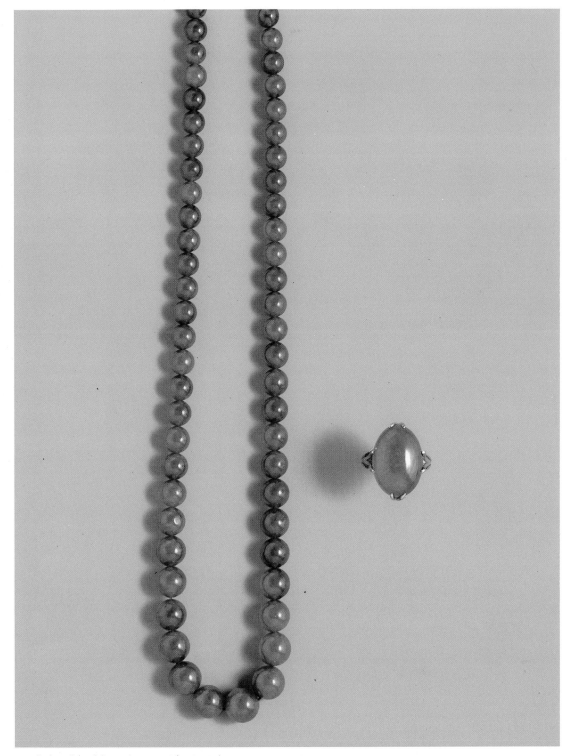

A jade bead necklace, $190,000 (£80,851)
A jade ring, $110,000 (£46,809)

The jewellery on this page was sold in New York on 17 October 1979

Centre, below and above A sapphire and diamond parure comprising a necklace, a
bracelet and a pair of pendent earrings, SFr 125,000 (£32,051:$75,321)
Left A marquise-shaped diamond ring, SFr 135,000 (£34,615:$81,346)
Right A sapphire and diamond ring, SFr 32,000 (£8,205:$19,282)

The jewellery on this page was sold in Zurich on 15 November 1979

An emerald bead and diamond necklace, HK $200,000 (£17,391:$40,870)
Above left An emerald and diamond ring, HK $21,000 (£1,826:$4,291)
Above right A ruby and diamond ring, HK $25,000 (£2,174:$5,109)
Centre A star ruby and diamond ring, HK $115,000 (£10,000:$23,500)
Below left A pair of emerald and diamond pendent earrings, HK $52,000 (£4,522:$10,626)
Below right A pair of emerald and diamond earrings, HK $92,000 (£8,000:$18,800)

The jewellery on this page was sold in Hong Kong on 3 December 1979

A pair of ruby and diamond cufflinks by
Van Cleef & Arpels
New York $17,500 (£7,447). 24.IV.80

Above A ruby and diamond brooch, the ruby weighing approximately 15.5 carats, *circa* 1920
New York $175,000 (£74,468). 18.X.79
Left A ruby and diamond ring, the ruby weighing approximately 11.5 carats
New York $310,000 (£131,915). 18.X.79
Centre A ruby and diamond ring by Van Cleef & Arpels, the ruby weighing approximately 11 carats
New York $305,000 (£129,787). 18.X.79
Right A ruby and diamond brooch, the rubies weighing approximately 8.8 carats
New York $90,000 (£38,298). 18.X.79

A ruby and diamond necklace by Cartier, the rubies weighing 28.51 carats,
SFr 450,000 (£115,385:$271,154)
A ruby and diamond ring, the ruby weighing 6.22 carats, SFr 140,000 (£35,897:$84,359)

The jewellery on this page was sold in Zurich on 8 May 1980

Above left The Honourable Artillery Company, Artillery Division, £460 ($1,081)
Above right The Queen's Royal Regiment (West Surrey), £300 ($705)
Centre The 1st The Queen's Dragoon Guards, £1,550 ($3,643)
Lower left The Grenadier Guards, £880 ($2,068)
Lower right The Scots Guards, £1,300 ($3,055)
Below centre The Suffolk Regiment, £500 ($1,175)

The regimental badge brooches in enamel, emeralds, rubies, sapphires and diamonds on this page
were sold in London on 27 September 1979

Glass and Paperweights

A *Nuppenbecher*, fourteenth century, height $3\frac{7}{8}$in (9.8cm)
London £16,000 ($37,600). 30.VI.80

Fig 1
A lead-glass coin goblet, enclosing a 1686 silver shilling,
circa 1686, height 9⅞in (25cm)
London £1,800 ($4,230). 28.IV.80

Fig 2
A commemorative wine glass, inscribed in relief
God Save ye King GR, *circa* 1715, height 6¼in (16cm)
London £1,800 ($4,230). 28.IV.80

English glass:
the Anthony Waugh Collection

R. J. Charleston

The classic conception of an English glass collection has been one in which drinking glasses – usually the best index of glass development – predominate to give a complete coverage of the differing styles that evolved through the eighteenth into the early nineteenth century. To these might be added as many seventeenth-century glasses as the collector had the luck to acquire (such things not being generally available for systematic collection), and eighteenth-century pieces of other shapes and types, such as blue glass with gilt and opaque-white glass with enamelled decoration. The Waugh Collection conformed in general to this prescription, which is justified by the main lines of English glass development as much as it is hallowed by tradition.

The classic seventeenth-century types owned by Anthony Waugh were represented by two large goblets. One has a globular knopped stem enclosing a 1686 shilling (Fig 1), and the other an elaborate 'figure-of-eight' stem, a survival into English lead-glass of a Venetian idiom. This glass was once in the D. H. Beves Collection, along with a contemporary decanter-jug, 'crizzled' in the seventeenth-century way. Like the coin goblet, it is decorated with mould-blown ribbing 'nipt diamond waies': over this have been laid vertical strips of glass, pinched in alternate horizontal and vertical projections with waffle-patterned tongs (*borsella puntata*). A similar repertory is found again on a charming small pocket flask, and Venetian ancestry shows in a slender-spouted small cruet – of lead-glass, despite its delicate appearance – with comparable tooled decoration.

From these rare and specialist pieces, the collection proceeded to the main series of eighteenth-century wine glasses, in which English glass-making finally found a style entirely its own. This begins with the evolution of the classic baluster glasses, in which the English glass-of-lead could finally display its intrinsic quality, uncluttered by decoration. These glasses have the knack of appearing monumental regardless of actual dimensions. They were well illustrated in Mr Waugh's collection, beginning with a noble inverted baluster goblet which adds actual size (11in) to its handsome proportions, and followed by splendid examples which ring the changes on the basic themes of globular and flattened knop, true and inverted baluster, with seemingly inexhaustible variety.

It is impossible here to detail the succeeding stem fashions – the pedestals, the air- and opaque-twists, mixed and coloured twists – but one or two highlights deserve mention. Among these was the wine glass with four-sided moulded pedestal stem inscribed with the words: *God Save ye King GR*, presumably commemorating George I's accession in 1714 (Fig 2). The colour-twist stems represented most known combinations, including the unusual and beautiful 'canary' yellow. There was also a series of engraved commemorative glasses, including the rare 'Duke of Cornwall Privateer'. Most impressive of all, however, were the glasses with Dutch wheel- and stippled point-engraving, notably a stipple-glass attributable to David Wolff at The Hague (Fig 3). Its exceptionally elegant chinoiseries probably identify it as the glass with 'A Chinaman playing a zither, as well as a boy playing with bells . . . very fine' in the Van Buren Sale of 1808, one of fourteen glasses ascribed to Wolff and described as 'of his best period'. Although this was perhaps the highpoint of the Waugh Collection, three further stipple-glasses, attributed to Wolff, J. van den Blijk and J. G. Smeyser respectively, were also strikingly interesting and attractive.

Fig 3
A detail of a chinoiserie goblet stipple-engraved by David Wolff, *circa* 1765, height 8½in (21.5cm)
London £10,500 ($24,675). 28.IV.80

An enamelled armorial *Stangenglas*, South German or
Venetian, 1570–90, height 11⅛in (28.3cm)
London £15,500 ($36,425). 30.VI.80

A Bohemian enamelled flask, 1661, height 10⅝in (27cm)
London £5,200 ($12,220). 30.VI.80

An amber pint-1 flask, circular medallion inscribed in relief *Jared Spencer*,
probably Pitkin Glass Works, East Manchester, Connecticut,
nineteenth century
Pokety Farms $22,000 (£9,362). 24.V.80
From the collection of the late Bernice Chrysler Garbisch

A cameo-glass vase by George Woodall, signed and inscribed on the base
UNDINE, *circa* 1885, height 11$\frac{3}{8}$in (28.8cm)
Belgravia £19,000 ($44,650). 20.IX.79

A French flower weight, diameter $3\frac{1}{8}$in (8.1cm)
£17,500 ($41,125)

A St Louis upright-bouquet basket weight, diameter 3in (7.8cm)
£15,000 ($35,250)
From the collection of Frank J. Manheim

The paperweights on this page were sold in London on 7 July 1980

Art Nouveau and Art Deco

An enamel and silver triptych, *The passing of Arthur*, by Phoebe Traquair, early twentieth century, height 8⅝in (22cm)
Belgravia £1,600 ($3,760). 7.XII.79

A glass vase with *marqueterie sur verre* and applied iridescent decoration by Emile Gallé,
circa 1902–1904, height 9in (23cm)
Monte Carlo FF 390,000 (£40,206:$94,485). 25.V.80

A carved cameo-glass marine vase with applied decoration by Emile Gallé, *circa* 1900,
height 8½in (21.5cm)
New York $37,500 (£15,957). 13.VI.80

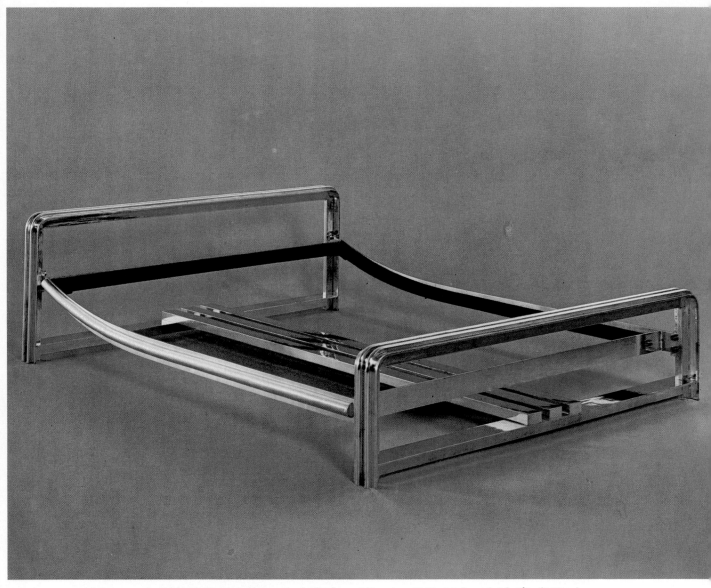

An aluminium double bed by Louis Sognot and Charlotte Alix, *circa* 1930–33, length 8ft 1½in (248cm)
Monte Carlo FF 560,000 (£57,732:$135,670). 25.V.80
From the collection of the late Maharaja of Indore

A black-painted and chromed metal chaise longue by Le Corbusier, 1928–29, length 5ft 2½in (159cm)
Monte Carlo FF 130,000 (£13,402:$31,495). 25.V.80
From the collection of the late Maharaja of Indore

Fig 1
A black lacquer screen by Eileen Gray, *circa* 1922–25, height 6ft 5½in (197cm)
Monte Carlo FF 130,000 (£13,402:$31,495). 25.V.80

Eileen Gray:
a pioneer of modern design

Philippe Garner

The event which sparked off a renewed interest in the work of Eileen Gray, resulting in the recent reappraisal of her career, was the sale of part of the collection of Jacques Doucet in Paris on 8 November 1972. The highlight of the auction was a magnificent lacquer screen by Miss Gray, 'Le destin', which established a new world record for twentieth-century furniture. Eileen Gray's reputation, so high in the 1920s and early '30s, had been eclipsed by that of other designers who were more aggressive in publicising their achievements. Miss Gray's modesty was such that, even ten years ago, her work was known only to very few. Although Eileen Gray lived to see the fashion for Art Deco and Modernism turn full circle, and to enjoy the first reawakening of interest in her own career, her death in 1976 denied her the final satisfaction of participating in the major retrospectives held in 1979 at the Victoria and Albert Museum, and in 1980 at the Museum of Modern Art, New York.

Eileen Gray was born in 1879 in Ireland. Her early career was remarkable for the courage and determination entailed in entering the Slade School of Art as one of its first women students and, subsequently, in settling alone in Paris in 1907, in the elegant Rue Bonaparte apartment which she was to occupy until her death. Most remarkable, however, was her decision to explore and practise the exacting craft of lacquer. This was in the years prior to the First World War, some time before lacquer came back into fashion as one of the popular materials of Art Deco furniture. Her chance, fortuitous beginnings are detailed in a letter written in June 1972:

> If you are still interested in lacquer, the answers to your questions are simple: it was just chance, that working at the Slade I saw a notice that in Charles workshop in Dean Street they repaired screens and things in lacquer. I . . . had been fascinated by that matière. Charles was very nice and said I might come and work there which I did. They used mostly coloured European varnishes to repair the old screens but also real lacquer from China, which I took to Paris meaning to work there . . . I had only time to do some base reliefs, Jacques Doucet wanted 'decorated lacquer frames' for his Van Goghs and Suzanne Talbot wanted big panels to cover the whole of her appartment . . . I think about 1913 Doucet bought a big screen ['Le destin'].

The first phase of Miss Gray's career was devoted to the creation of luxurious furniture and decorations in lacquer, and in Jacques Doucet and Suzanne Talbot she found two of her most important early patrons. She created relatively few works for Doucet but each one is a masterpiece, in both conception and execution. For Suzanne Talbot, the professional name of Mme Mathieu Lévy, she spent three years, from 1919, redecorating an apartment and it was for this scheme that she first devised the block screens which are perhaps the best known and certainly among the most interesting of her designs. Two such screens, one in black lacquer (Fig 1) and one in white-painted wood, furnished her own home. In 1922 Eileen Gray opened a showroom in the Rue du Faubourg St Honoré, calling it the Galerie Jean Désert. Here she showed and sold lacquer furniture, carpets, lamps and other furnishings. She ran the gallery until 1930, but, even at the time of its inception, Jean Désert represented a phase in her career which had a limited future. Her own development was rapidly leading her away from luxury furnishings to a new functionalism, which first manifested itself in the early 1920s and which, by the close of the decade, had become Miss Gray's exclusive preoccupation. Early and instinctively she followed a path that was to become a major international trend with the emergence in the late 1920s of the Modernist style.

A turning point in Eileen Gray's stylistic development was her cool, spacious and relatively austere project for a 'bedroom-boudoir for Monte Carlo' presented in 1923 at the Salon des Artistes Décorateurs. The scheme met with the disapprobation of French critics who were not in tune with its minimalism, but it attracted the attention of J. J. P. Oud, a leading figure of the Dutch avant-garde *De Stijl* group, who eagerly made contact with Miss Gray. Since the previous year she had also been in correspondence with another member of the Dutch group, Jan Wils, and this refreshing new influence on her work was reflected in the design of a remarkable table of 1922 (Fig 2), a sculptural interplay of horizontal and vertical planes which payed tribute to the formal concerns of the *De Stijl* group. In 1924 the Dutch in turn payed homage to Miss Gray's Modernism, devoting an entire issue of the art journal *Wendingen* to her work.

Abandoning lacquer, Eileen Gray discovered a host of new materials which she was to exploit with inventiveness and flair through the late 1920s and '30s. Many of these materials would lend themselves easily to the series production of her designs, though in fact most of her ideas were implemented only in small numbers, either in prototype form for her own use, or for specific interiors or projects. She used various metals including aluminium, chromium-plated tubular steel and perforated sheet metal, in conjunction, most dramatically, with new synthetics as in the tall metal-framed celluloid screen which graced her Rue Bonaparte sitting room. Her inquiring mind sought not just novelty of materials but practical new ideas of furniture construction, such as pivoting elements and knock-down structure, which are as fresh and relevant today as when first conceived some fifty years ago. Eileen Gray has justly earned her place as a pioneer of modern design.

Fig 2
A painted sycamore and oak table by Eileen Gray in the style of the *De Stijl* group, 1922,
width 2ft 1$\frac{5}{8}$in (65cm)
Monte Carlo FF 160,000 (£16,495:$38,763). 25.V.80

A Rozenburg 'eggshell' vase, decorated by Sam Schellink, 1906,
height $16\frac{3}{8}$in (41.5cm)
Belgravia £5,000 ($11,750). 26.IX.79

Coins and Medals

Left The Most Honourable Order of the Bath (GCB)
Top row, left to right Waterloo medal, Military General Service medal, Russian Order of St Anne
Bottom row, left and right Peninsular Gold Cross, Field Officer's gold medal
Right Field Marshal's baton

Field Marshal Sir William Maynard Gomm, GCB, to whom these medals were awarded, was born in Barbados in 1784. He was gazetted an Ensign in the 9th Foot at the age of only ten, as a result of his father's gallant death in battle in 1794. After a distinguished military career, he occupied numerous ceremonial posts, and died in 1875, having held the longest continuous commission in the history of the British Army

The military insignia on this page were part of a lot sold in London on 5 March 1980 for £26,000 ($61,100)

ANCIENT GREEK, tetradrachm of Carthage,
circa 320 BC
London £2,100 ($4,935). 20.II.80

ROMAN, solidus of Magnus
Maximus (383–88 AD)
London £2,600 ($6,110).
15.VII.80

ITALY, Piacenza, 2 doppie of Odoardo
Farnese, 1626
London £1,700 ($3,995). 20.II.80

CHINA, bronze knife money, late Zhou
Dynasty (*circa* 770–400 BC)
London £420 ($987). 23.I.80

Reduced

ENGLAND, pound of Elizabeth I, mint mark woolpack
(1594–96)
London £4,000 ($9,400). 11.VI.80

FRANCE, pavillion d'or of Philip VI (1328–50)
London £2,100 ($4,935). 11.VI.80

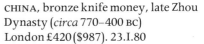

ENGLAND, crown of William and Mary, 1692
London £1,800 ($4,230). 16.IV.80

ENGLAND, crown of Queen Anne, 1703, *VIGO* below bust
London £1,700 ($3,995). 16.IV.80

UNITED STATES OF AMERICA, half-dollar, 1862
London £1,400 ($3,290). 11.VI.80

ZANZIBAR, 2½ rials of Barghash
ibn Sa'id, AH 1299 (1881 AD)
London £10,000 ($23,500).
23.IV.80

UNITED STATES OF AMERICA, Panama-Pacific Exposition, octagonal
50 dollars, 1915
New York $42,000 (£17,872). 8.VII.80

AUSTRALIA, Sydney Mint
sovereign of Victoria, 1856
London £3,100 ($7,285). 11.VI.80

ENGLAND, Royal Mint model of
the proposed nickel-brass
threepence of Edward VIII, 1937
London £4,000 ($9,400). 9.X.79

AUSTRIA, Maria Theresia, gold prize medal for agriculture, 1765, by Anton Widemann
London £2,600 ($6,110). 16.IV.80

ITALY, bronze portrait medal of Leonello D'Este, Marquess of Ferrara
(1441–50), by Amadio da Milano
London £1,000 ($2,350). 23.I.80

UNITED STATES OF AMERICA, gold life-saving medal of the first class, Act of
Congress 20 June 1874, awarded to Captain Frederick Kendrick
New York $8,500 (£3,617). 9.VI.80

Photographs

CECIL BEATON
Marilyn Monroe
Silver print, signed, inscribed with the title and stamped with the photographer's credit on the reverse, 1956, 14in by 11in (35.5cm by 28cm)
Belgravia £420 ($987). 26.X.79

NADAR (GASPARD FELIX TOURNACHON)
Portrait of Alexandre Dumas, père
Salt print, signed and inscribed *113 St. Lazare*, 1857, 9$\frac{3}{8}$in by 7$\frac{1}{4}$in (24cm by 18.5cm)
New York $16,000 (£6,809). 2.XI.79

DAVID HOCKNEY
Still life with hats
C-type print, signed and numbered *6/80*, 1973, 9⅜in by 7in (24cm by 18cm)
New York $900 (£383). 20.V.80

HELMUT NEWTON
Veruschka in Nice
Silver print, signed and dated *1975*, 28in by 43¼in (71cm by 110cm)
New York $1,600(£681). 2.XI.79
From the collection of Joseph Macdonald

Arms and Armour

A *czapka* by F. A. Stone & Sons, from an officer's uniform of the 16th The Queen's Lancers, *circa* 1914
London £1,050 ($2,468). 30.X.79

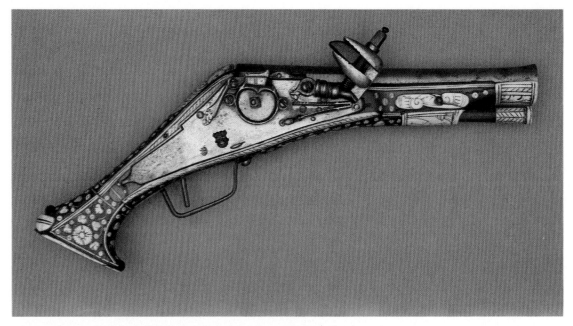

A Nuremberg wheel-lock dag, late sixteenth century, length 14½in (37cm)
London £4,800 ($11,280). 1.IV.80

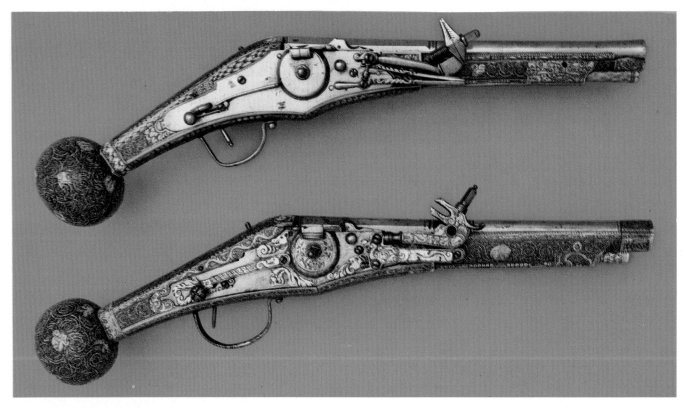

Above A Saxon wheel-lock dag, late sixteenth century, length 12¾in (32.5cm)
Los Angeles $23,500 (£10,000). 20.IV.80
Below A Saxon wheel-lock dag, dated *1595*, length 12½in (32cm)
Los Angeles $40,000 (£17,021). 20.IV.80

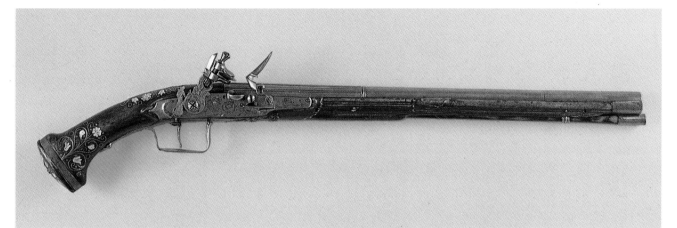

A German flintlock three-shot superimposed-load doglock holster pistol, mid seventeenth century,
length 17½in (44.5cm)
Los Angeles $26,000 (£11,064). 16.IX.79

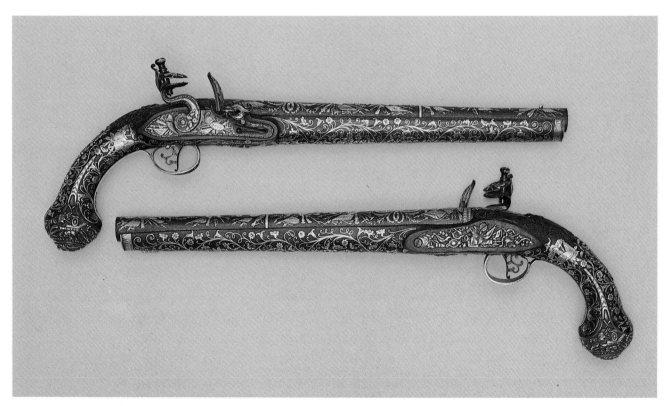

A pair of silver-mounted presentation flintlock holster pistols by H. W. Mortimer, London, 1790,
length 19in (48.5cm)
London £15,000 ($35,250). 17.VI.80

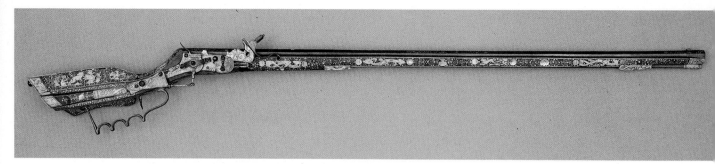

A Silesian wheel-lock *tschinke*, *circa* 1630, length 46in (117cm)
£4,600 ($10,810)

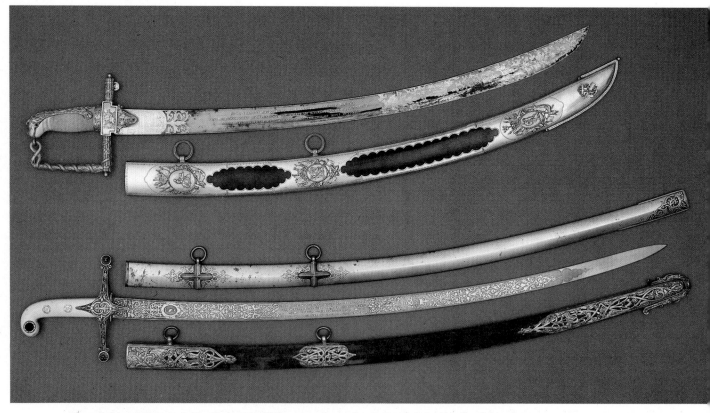

Above A Lloyds Patriotic Fund sword of fifty pound type by R. Teed, inscribed and dated *1811*,
length 35½in (90cm)
£6,400 ($15,040)
Below A silver-gilt-mounted presentation Mamluke officer's sword of Australian interest by
Henry Wilkinson, serial number 11768, inscribed and dated *1862*, length 39⅜in (100cm)
£1,900 ($4,465)

The arms on this page were sold in London on 22 April 1980

Clocks
and
Watches

An ormolu-mounted walnut marquetry
quarter-striking bracket clock by
Aimé Ducommun, *circa* 1790, height
37in (94cm)
Zurich SFr 42,000 (£10,769:$25,308).
13.XI.79

An alarum day and night clock by John Hilderson, London, *circa* 1665, height 21½in (54.5cm)
London £18,000 ($42,300). 25.X.79
From the collection of the late W. G. Barnes

A silver-mounted tortoise-shell musical bracket clock by Simon Des Charmes, London, *circa* 1725,
height $31\frac{1}{2}$in (80cm)
New York $65,000 (£27,660). 27.X.79

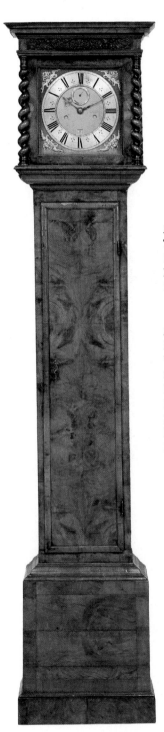

Left A walnut longcase clock by
Thomas Tompion, London, *circa*
1680, height 6ft 5in (196cm)
London £23,000 ($54,050).
1.V.80

Right A Federal inlaid mahogany
longcase clock by Caleb
Wheaton, the case by Ichabod
Sanford and dated *1796*,
height 8ft (244cm)
New York $75,000 (£31,915).
2.II.80
From the collection of the late
Mr and Mrs William B. Hysan Jr

Left J. N. ADORNO NO 1
A gold and enamel double-dialled two train minute-repeating geographical and astronomical watch, Mexico and London, *circa* 1890, diameter $2\frac{1}{8}$in (5.4cm)
New York $75,000 (£31,915). 11.VI.80

Right A gold and enamel pair cased pocket chronometer by William Ilbery, London, 1813, diameter $2\frac{3}{8}$in (6cm)
New York $21,000 (£8,936). 27.X.79

Left A gold and enamel hunting cased double-dialled minute-repeating automaton calendar watch for the Oriental market by L. Vrard & Co, *circa* 1890, diameter $2\frac{3}{8}$in (6cm)
New York $60,000 (£25,532). 11.VI.80

A gold and enamel pair cased watch and chatelaine by L'Epine, *circa* 1790, diameter $2\frac{1}{2}$in (6.4cm)
New York $15,500 (£6,596). 16.IV.80

A silver and gilt-metal cruciform watch by Abraham Cusin, Nevers, early seventeenth century, length 1¾in (4.5cm) London £42,000 ($98,700). 29.XI.79 From the Belin Collection

A gold and agate centre seconds duplex watch for the Chinese market by William Ilbery, London, early nineteenth century, length 3⅞in (9.9cm) London £28,000 ($65,800). 29.XI.79 From the Belin Collection

A gold and enamel pair cased verge watch by Charles Bobinet, *circa* 1640, diameter 1½in (3.9cm) London £44,000 ($103,400). 29.XI.79 From the Belin Collection

DANIEL QUARE NO 391
A gold pair cased quarter-repeating verge watch, *circa* 1700, diameter 2¼in (5.6cm) London £13,500 ($31,725). 29.XI.79 From the Belin Collection

MARGETTS NO 1253
A gold pair cased pocket chronometer, 1800, diameter 2¼in (5.6cm) London £11,000 ($25,850). 25.X.79

WILLIAM ANTHONY NO 1705
A gold, enamel and pearl
watch with expanding and
contracting hands, *circa* 1810,
length 3½in (8.8cm)
London £72,000 ($169,200).
29.XI.79
From the Belin Collection

Right A gold and enamel
centre seconds duplex watch,
by Stedman & Vardon,
London, 1791, diameter 2½in
(6.4cm)
London £28,000 ($65,800).
29.XI.79
From the Belin Collection

A gold and enamel quarter-
repeating centre seconds musical
automaton watch by Fd. Aubert,
early nineteenth century,
diameter 2⅛in (5.5cm)
Zurich SFr140,000
(£35,897:$84,359). 13.XI.79

Left and right Two views of a
gold cased *tourbillon* watch by
E. Buffat, the hour markings
spelling *Napoleon III* and the
wheel bridges arranged to form
the letter *N, circa* 1860, diameter
2in (5.2cm)
London £40,000 ($94,000).
29.XI.79
From the Belin Collection

GEORGE COWLE NO 342
A gold cased presentation pocket chronometer, 1827, diameter 2½in (6.4cm)
Zurich SFr 70,000 (£17,949:$42,179). 13.XI.79
From the collection of the late Sam Bloomfield

Right BREGUET NO 452
A gold cased two-barrel lever watch, mid nineteenth century, diameter 2in (5.2cm)
London £25,000 ($58,750). 29.XI.79
From the Belin Collection

HUNT & ROSKELL NO 10413
A gold *montre à tact*, 1848, diameter 2⅛in (5.4cm)
Zurich SFr 125,000 (£32,051:$75,321). 13.XI.79
From the collection of the late Sam Bloomfield

THOMAS CUMMINS NO 14 = 26
A gold lever watch, 1825, diameter 2⅛in (5.4cm)
London £23,000 ($54,050). 29.XI.79
From the Belin Collection

VICTOR KULLBERG NO 7108
A gold cased split seconds minute-repeating fusee keyless lever watch, 1901, diameter 2⅝in (6.6cm)
Zurich SFr 100,000 (£25,641:$60,256). 13.XI.79
From the collection of the late Sam Bloomfield

Musical Instruments

A pianoforte by William Southwell, Dublin, inscribed on the nameboard *Southwell fecit, circa* 1785,
length 5ft 2¾in (159.5cm)
London £18,500 ($43,475). 20.III.80

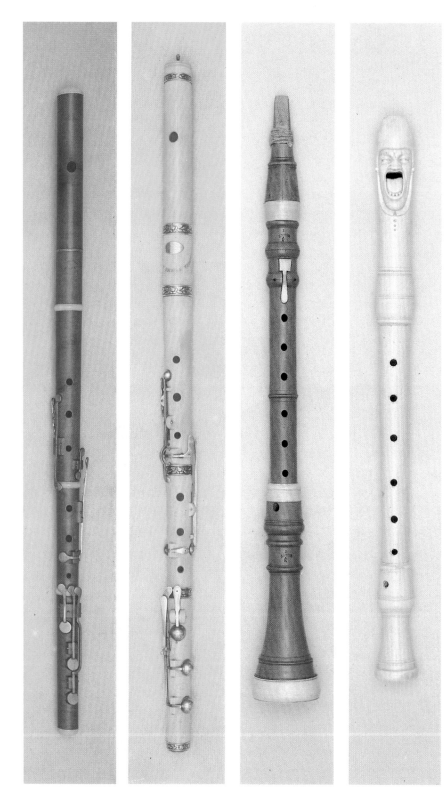

From left to right
An eight-keyed boxwood flute
by Theobald Boehm & Rodol
Greve, Munich, stamped
Boehm & Greve a Munich, *circa*
1828, sounding length 23in
(58.5cm)
London £3,400 ($7,990).
8.XI.79

An eight-keyed ivory flute by
Cornelius Ward, London,
stamped *Corns. Ward, London*,
circa 1830, sounding
length $23\frac{3}{16}$ in (59cm)
London £1,700 ($3,995).
8.XI.79
From the collection of James
MacGillivray

A two-keyed boxwood clarinet
in D by I. Scherer, Paris,
stamped *Scherer*, *circa* 1750,
length $20\frac{1}{4}$ in (51.5cm)
London £5,000 ($11,750).
22.V.80

An ivory alto recorder, German
or Dutch, *circa* 1730,
length 19in (48.5cm)
London £2,300 ($5,405).
22.V.80

A bass viola da gamba by Barak
Norman, London, 1700, labelled *Barak
Norman at the Bass Violl in St. Pauls
Ally, London, fecit 1700*, length of back
$26\frac{13}{16}$ in (68cm)
London £12,000 ($28,200). 22.V.80

A Flemish virginals by Cornelius Hagaerts, Antwerp, inscribed on the jackrail *Cornelius Hagaerts me fecit Antwerpiae, circa* 1630, length 4ft 9⅛in (145cm)
London £14,000 ($32,900). 22.V.80

A violin by Francesco Rugeri, Cremona, 1696,
labelled *Francesco Rugeri detto il per in Cremona
1696*, length of back 14in (35.5cm)
London £27,000 ($63,450). 22.V.80

The Regnier, a violin by Antonio Stradivari, Cremona,
1727, labelled *Antonius Stradiuarius Cremonensis
faciebat Anno 1727*, length of back $13\frac{15}{16}$in (35.5cm)
London £96,000 ($225,600). 18.X.79

A 'portable grand pianoforte' by John Isaac Hawkins, London, inscribed on the nameboard *John I. Hawkins, Inventor & Patentee, Dalby Terrace, City Road, London*, after 1803, height 4ft 6¾in (139cm)
London £7,400 ($17,390). 20.III.80
From the collection of John Broadwood & Sons

Furniture, Decorations and Textiles

A Steinway grand piano and a pair of stools designed by Sir Lawrence Alma-Tadema, RA, 1884–87,
the faciaboard painted by Sir Edward J. Poynter, PRA, signed and dated *1887*
PB Eighty-four $390,000 (£165,957). 26.III.80
From the collection of the Martin Beck Theatre

A Louis XV marquetry writing table stamped *Delorme*, *circa* 1750, width 2ft 4½in (72.5cm)
London £15,000 ($35,250). 11.VII.80

Adrien Delorme was received Master in 1748

A Louis XV ormolu-mounted tulipwood and fruitwood marquetry *table en chiffonière* stamped I. *Dubois,* by Jacques or René Dubois, *circa* 1745, width 1ft 5in (43cm) New York $42,500 (£18,085). 17.V.80
From the collection of the late Bernice Chrysler Garbisch

Jacques Dubois was received Master in 1742 and his son René was received Master in 1755

A Louis XV ormolu-mounted marquetry writing table stamped *J. Dautriche, circa* 1770,
width 2ft 8¼in (82cm)
Monte Carlo FF 750,000 (£77,320 : $181,701). 25.XI.79
From the collection of Claude Cartier

Jacques Dautriche was received Master in 1765

A Louis XIV ormolu-mounted purplewood and ebony commode, early eighteenth century,
width 4ft 3½in (131cm)
New York $39,000 (£16,596). 12.IV.80

A Louis XV ormolu-mounted tulipwood parquetry commode attributed to Charles Cressent, second quarter eighteenth century, width 4ft 11in (150cm)
New York $165,000 (£70,213). 17.V.80
From the collection of the late Bernice Chrysler Garbisch

One of a pair of Louis XV gilt-wood chairs made for Madame du Barry by Delanois, 1769
Monte Carlo FF 600,000 (£61,856 : $145,361). 26.V.80
From the collection of Mme Lopez-Willshaw

Louis Delanois was received Master in 1761

One of a pair of Louis XVI ormolu-mounted porcelain
pots-pourris, *circa* 1775, height 1ft 5¼in (44cm)
Monte Carlo FF120,000 (£12,371 : $29,072). 27.V.80

One of a pair of late Louis XV ormolu fire-dogs attributed to Quentin-Claude Pitoin, *circa* 1772,
length 2ft 4¾in (73cm)
Monte Carlo FF 360,000 (£37,113 : $87,216). 26.V.80

A Louis XVI marble, bronze and ormolu clock after a design by Pierre-Philippe Thomire, *circa* 1785, width 2ft ¾in (63cm)
Monte Carlo FF400,000 (£41,237 : $96,907). 26.V.80
From the collection of the Comtesse de Bismarck

A palisander and *pietra dura* table
cabinet, Florence or Prague,
circa 1680, width 3ft 2in (96.5cm)
London £20,000 ($47,000).
18.VII.80

A mother-of-pearl-inlaid tortoise-shell table attributed to Pieter de Loose and Michel Verbiest,
Antwerp, *circa* 1680, width 4ft 9½in (146cm)
Monte Carlo FF 430,000 (£44,330 : $104,175). 28.X.79
From the collection of His Highness Prince Sadruddin Aga Khan

A German Neo-classical ormolu-mounted mahogany cylinder desk in the manner of David Roentgen, late eighteenth century, height 5ft 5in (165cm)
New York $55,000 (£23,404). 12. IV.80

David Roentgen was received Master in 1780

One of a pair of engraved and blue glass gilt-wood mirrors, Venice, early
eighteenth century, height 4ft 4¾in (133cm)
Monte Carlo FF 290,000 (£29,897 : $70,258). 26.V.80

A Queen Anne mulberry wood double-domed bureau bookcase attributed to G. Coxed and T. Woster, *circa* 1715, height 6ft 10½in (209.5cm)
New York $48,000 (£20,426). 26.IV.80
From the collection of the late Gertrude B. Levin

One of a set of six George II mahogany dining chairs
attributed to Thomas Chippendale, *circa* 1755
New York $45,000 (£19,149). 26.IV.80
From the collection of the late Mabel Brady Garvan

One of a set of six George I walnut dining chairs,
circa 1725
New York $26,000 (£11,064). 27.X.79

A George II brass-inlaid padouk bureau cabinet in the manner of John Channon, *circa* 1735, height 7ft 11in (241.5cm)
New York $21,000 (£8,936). 26.IV.80

One of a pair of George III marquetry commodes attributed to William Moore, Dublin, *circa* 1780,
width 4ft 5in (134.5cm)
London £31,000 ($72,850). 23.XI.79
From the collection of the late the Hon. Mrs E. W. H. Eliot

A George III ormolu-mounted commode attributed to Pierre Langlois, *circa* 1760, width 5ft 1in (155cm)
London £120,000 ($282,000). 23.XI.79

Fig 1
A Chippendale Cuban mahogany block-front and shell-carved kneehole desk attributed to
Edmund Townsend, Newport, Rhode Island, *circa* 1770, width 3ft ½in (93cm)
Pokety Farms $250,000 (£106,383). 24.V.80
From the collection of the late Bernice Chrysler Garbisch

American furniture:
a new era of collecting

William W. Stahl Jr

The Girl Scouts Loan Exhibition of Eighteenth and Early Nineteenth Century Furniture and Glass, which opened at the American Arts Association on 29 September 1929, marked the recognition of the quality of the arts produced in the early years of America's history. The exhibition, with its highly illustrated catalogue, encouraged a new generation of collectors and scholars, which resulted in the formation of major museum and private collections, and the development of a strong market.

During the first half of 1980, a series of events unparalleled in the history of American decorative arts collecting took place: In Praise of America, a recreation of the 1929 Girl Scouts Loan Exhibition, was held at the National Gallery in Washington DC, their first exhibition devoted to the decorative arts; the American Wing at the Metropolitan Museum, which has been closed for nearly a decade, was reopened; Yale University held a special exhibition to commemorate Francis P. Garvan's gift of American furniture and related decorative arts, bequeathed to the University Art Gallery, in his wife's honour, in 1930; the centenary of the birth of the late Henry Francis du Pont was celebrated in recognition of the enormous contribution he made by turning his residence, Winterthur, into a learning centre and museum; and two significant collections of American furniture and decorative arts – those of the Garvan and Garbisch families – were dispersed. At a time when scholarship in the area was minimal, both the Garvans and Garbisches amassed vast and diverse collections which exerted a strong influence on the field, and both gave major portions of their collections to museums.

Francis P. and Mabel Brady Garvan were among those 'pioneer' collectors who sponsored the original Girl Scouts Exhibition. Numerous items illustrated in Wallace Nutting's *Furniture Treasury* (1928), one of the first attempts at documenting American furniture forms, were owned by them. They purchased on a grand scale, filling a New York apartment; a house in Millbrook, New York; Kamp Kill Kare, their Adirondack Mountain retreat; and a warehouse in New York City to store the surplus. It is largely due to the Garvans' contributions that the Yale University Art Gallery has become a centre for the study of American art.

The Garvans were interested in all types of American furniture and related

Fig 2
A Chippendale walnut lowboy, Philadelphia, Pennsylvania, 1755–80, width 2ft 10¼in (87cm)
New York $63,000(£26,809). 7.VI.80
From the collection of the late Mabel Brady Garvan

decorative arts, from the Pilgrim century to the Federal period. One of the most significant examples of American furniture in their collection was a Salem, Massachusetts, block-front chest-on-chest (Fig 3). It is similar to another chest-on-chest, attributed to Nathaniel Treadwell of Beverly, Massachusetts, donated by Francis P. Garvan to Yale as part of his 1930 gift. Both pieces have an enclosed bonnet and a fan motif in the centre drawer, flanked by upward-curving small drawers. The drawers in the upper section are in turn flanked by fluted pilasters. These characteristics are typical of chests produced north of Boston during the second half of the eighteenth century. The distinctive Salem features are the two pinwheel motifs carved on the crest. Massachusetts block-front furniture was made from the 1730s until as late as

Fig 3
A Chippendale mahogany bonnet-top block-front chest-on-chest, Salem,
Massachusetts, *circa* 1775, height 7ft 5$\frac{1}{4}$in (227cm)
New York $39,000 (£16,596). 7.VI.80
From the collection of the late Mabel Brady Garvan

1800, both in urban centres, such as Boston and nearby Charlestown, and in the outlying regions of Salem, Beverly and Concord. Few documented examples exist, however, and only about half a dozen bearing signatures or with records of provenance have survived. The Garvan chest has the inscription *William Hale (Hall?) Boston* in several places on the lower section, indicating that Hall was an owner, rather than a maker, since the style of the piece is distinctively 'north of Boston'.

The Garvans' Massachusetts serpentine-front chest was another example of a major case piece from New England, this one attributed to Elijah Sanderson, who worked in Salem until about 1810. Sanderson was a prolific maker, and his papers at the Essex Institute in Salem show that as early as 1803 he shipped furniture to many parts of the American South, Brazil, and the East and West Indies. His long career included an association with Samuel McIntire, the noted architect and wood carver of Salem. In the Garvan chest, with its strong, broad, chamfered front corners which continue down to related ogee bracket feet, the bulkiness of American Chippendale style is still apparent, while the serpentine front and the top shaped to rounded front corners, are features found in tables of the classical revival period.

In 1929, the Garvans loaned a fine Philadelphia lowboy (Fig 2) to the Girl Scouts Exhibition (no 642 in the exhibition catalogue), which was among those pieces chosen by Wallace Nutting to illustrate his *Furniture Treasury*. This work relates to a large group of lowboys or dressing tables, which were sometimes made as companion pieces to high chests of drawers. Its broad proportions, use of walnut as a primary wood, classic detailing in the form of a recessed shell surrounded by applied carved grasses and finely shaped skirt, are all hallmarks of Pennsylvania design.

Edgar William and Bernice Chrysler Garbisch were best known as collectors of American naive paintings, a term Colonel Garbisch coined to describe non-academic American paintings. They formed the painting collection with the intention of offering it to the nation, and it ultimately benefited the National Gallery, Washington DC, the Metropolitan Museum, the Philadelphia Museum of Art and other institutions. Through American Naive Paintings of the 18th and 19th Centuries, the 1968/70 travelling exhibition of 111 masterpieces from their collection, all America and a large part of Europe and Japan were introduced to this unfamiliar art form. It was at Pokety Farms, on Maryland's eastern shore, their country residence for more than thirty years, that the Garbisches concentrated on forming a collection of decorative arts, with a special emphasis on furniture associated with specific cabinet-makers.

Some of the most distinctive furniture produced in America originated in Connecticut during the eighteenth century. Typical of this period is a pair of side chairs made by Eliphalet Chapin, who worked in East Windsor, Connecticut, until about 1780. The chairs are unusual because they are constructed of mahogany rather than the more common native cherrywood. (An almost identical pair of Chapin chairs made of cherry – the primary wood favoured by Connecticut craftsmen because of its local availability – was owned by Mrs Garvan.) Having trained in Connecticut, Chapin spent about three years in Philadelphia before returning to East Windsor. Although some of his design and construction techniques show the obvious influence of his Philadelphia training, Chapin also borrowed design features from other regions. The

Fig 4
A Chippendale mahogany *bombé* chest of drawers, Massachusetts, 1760–80, width 2ft 11½in (90cm)
Pokety Farms $160,000 (£68,085). 24.V.80
From the collection of the late Bernice Chrysler Garbisch

result was a highly distinctive, if eclectic, style. The shape of the crestrail and carved centre shell, and the formation of the legs and feet are signatures of his work.

The Garbisches' collection of children's and miniature furniture, including spice chests, numbered thirty pieces. Two of the most interesting examples, both of Pennsylvania origin, were a miniature highboy and a spice cabinet in the form of a miniature highboy. The first, of classic William and Mary design, can be ascribed to Chester County, on the basis of its turnings, its panelled sides and the use of native walnut favoured in that region. While the basic design indicates that it was made about 1710, it could date as late as 1750 because popular styles did linger on, particularly in areas outside major cabinet-making centres. The mahogany spice cabinet (Fig 5), from Lancaster County, is constructed in the shape of a highboy, and was meant to sit on a shelf. The top was left unfinished for this reason, and it was also hidden by a finely carved scrollboard centred by a shell- and vine-carved ornament. Behind the pair of cupboard doors is an arrangement of thirteen small drawers. The design of this cabinet is related to a group of shelf-clocks with Lancaster provenance, all of which have similar proportions and delicately carved decoration.

American *bombé* furniture is rare, well designed, skilfully constructed and one of the most outstanding forms produced by eighteenth-century craftsmen. The Garbisch Massachusetts chest of drawers exhibits compact proportions, choice mahogany and colour, and fine original brasses. The chest (Fig 4) is part of a group of *bombé* furniture which includes slant-front desks, desks-and-bookcases, chests-on-chests and dressing glasses. The survival of this group is important as production was almost exclusively confined to the city of Boston and its immediate environs, during the third quarter of the eighteenth century.

Another New England furniture form was illustrated by a porringer-top tea table with candleslides. Tea tables were produced in virtually every part of eighteenth-century America. The Garbisch table is the only known example that combines a rectangular top with porringer ends, and with the rare feature of candleslides or rests. Normally, a tea table with porringer top is associated with Rhode Island, but given the fluid exchange of ideas between Connecticut and Rhode Island, it was probably produced in eastern Connecticut, or very near the Rhode Island border. Connecticut furniture makers thought nothing of combining elements from various classic designs. The results were often masterpieces, as is this tea table, with its shaped top, gracefully scalloped skirt, high delicate cabriole legs and tall pad feet.

The most important single piece of furniture in this collection was the Newport, Rhode Island, block-front and shell-carved kneehole desk or dressing table (Fig 1), made about 1770, probably by Edmund Townsend. The basic form, a combination of the kneehole desk with block-front drawers and decorative motifs of convex and concave shells, is peculiar to Rhode Island and is unlike any other furniture produced at that time. It has long been considered the *ne plus ultra* of American design and construction. The Garbisch example is one of about fifteen known pieces, and typifies the finest Newport cabinetwork. The various members of the Goddard-Townsend family, who all worked in Newport from about 1730 until the early nineteenth century, were among the first American cabinet-makers to be identified and recognised for the near perfect balance and proportions of their work.

Fig 5
A Chippendale mahogany spice cabinet in the form of a miniature highboy, Lancaster
County, Pennsylvania, 1760–80, height 3ft 10¾in (119cm)
Pokety Farms $36,000 (£15,319). 24.V.80
From the collection of the late Bernice Chrysler Garbisch

Francis P. Garvan's purpose throughout his collecting career, which culminated with his gift to Yale, was to 'educate America' in the quality and range of the arts produced during the formative years of the nation. This spirit, shared by the Garbisches, has inspired another generation of collectors and has helped raise the arts of America to their present standing.

One of a pair of Chippendale walnut side chairs attributed
to Thomas Affleck, Philadelphia, 1760–80
New York $70,000 (£29,787). 3.V.80

One of a pair of Chippendale mahogany side chairs attributed to
Eliphalet Chapin, East Windsor, Connecticut, 1775–85
Pokety Farms $29,000 (£12,340). 24.V.80
From the collection of the late Bernice Chrysler Garbisch

A Chippendale mahogany wing armchair, Philadelphia, 1765–80
Pokety Farms $62,500 (£26,596). 24.V.80
From the collection of the late Bernice Chrysler Garbisch

A Chippendale mahogany serpentine-front chest of drawers attributed to Elijah Sanderson, Salem,
Massachusetts, 1785–90, width 3ft 5$\frac{1}{4}$in (105cm)
New York $36,000 (£15,319). 7.VI.80
From the collection of the late Mabel Brady Garvan

A Queen Anne mahogany porringer-top tea table with candleslides, Connecticut or Rhode Island,
1740–55, width 2ft 8in (81.5cm)
Pokety Farms $56,000 (£23,830). 24.V.80
From the collection of the late Bernice Chrysler Garbisch

A Queen Anne cherrywood bonnet-top highboy by Jonathan Brooks, New London,
Connecticut, signed *John Brooks* and dated *1769*, height 7ft 5¼in (227cm)
New York $40,000 (£17,021). 1.XII.79
From the collection of A. T. Seaver

A Federal inlaid mahogany and satinwood tambour desk and bookcase attributed to John and Thomas Seymour, Boston, Massachusetts, *circa* 1800, height 5ft 10in (178cm)
Pokety Farms $39,000 (£16,596). 24.V.80
From the collection of the late Bernice Chrysler Garbisch

A Second Empire ormolu and *verde antico* marble centre table, *circa* 1865,
height 2ft 6¾in (78cm)
Monte Carlo FF 50,000 (£5,155 : $12,113). 26.XI.79

The stamp *TUIL*. with a crowned *N* suggests that this table was in the collection of
Napoleon III at the Tuileries

A Louis XIV style ormolu-mounted pewter and brass tortoise-shell and ebony cabinet-on-stand, stamped *F. Linke*, after André-Charles Boulle, *circa* 1900, height 6ft 3in (190.5cm)
Los Angeles $21,000 (£8,936). 6.XI.79

One of a pair of French ormolu-mounted harewood and marquetry commodes, *circa* 1900, width 3ft 10in (117cm)
£7,800 ($18,330)

A French ormolu-mounted mahogany and marquetry commode, *circa* 1900, width 5ft 4¾in (164.5cm)
£5,000 ($11,750)

The commodes on this page were sold at Belgravia on 2 April 1980

An ormolu regulator in the style of
Caffiéri, Paris, mid nineteenth century,
height 6ft 5⅞in (198cm)
Monte Carlo FF190,000(£19,588:$46,031).
26.XI.79
From the collection of Miss Layton

This regulator is a copy of the one made
by Passemant for Louis XV at Versailles

One of a pair of French ormolu-mounted tulipwood display cabinets, *circa* 1900, height 4ft 11½in (151cm)
Belgravia £5,500 ($12,925). 2.IV.80

A painted and ormolu purplehart centre table stamped
A. Beurdeley à Paris, circa 1870, height 2ft 9in (84cm)
Monte Carlo FF110,000 (£11,340 : $26,649). 26.XI.79

A Brussels tapestry of Theseus dancing before the temple of Apollo, Delos, from the series *Les hommes illustres d'après Plutarque*, by Urbanus and Daniel Leyniers and Henry II Reydams after Victor Janssens, early eighteenth century, 12ft 9in by 14ft 10in (389cm by 452.5cm)
London £16,000 ($37,600). 18.VII.80

A late Gothic Tournai falconry tapestry, early sixteenth century, 10ft 8in by 13ft 9in
(325.5cm by 419.5cm)
London £125,000 ($293,750). 17.IV.80

An English 'Turkeywork' carpet, *circa* 1620, 17ft by 7ft 11in
(518.5cm by 241.5cm)
London £100,000 ($235,000). 17.IV.80
From the collection of the late 16th Earl of Strathmore

A dragon carpet, seventeenth century, 6ft 3in by 12ft 10in
(190.5cm by 391.5cm)
London £12,500 ($29,375). 23.IV.80

An Heriz silk carpet, *circa* 1880, 9ft by 6ft 2in (274.5cm by 188cm)
New York $67,500 (£28,723). 15.XII.79

A double-sided Kashan wool and silk prayer rug, nineteenth century,
7ft 11in by 4ft 10in (241.5cm by 147.5cm)
London £14,500 ($34,075). 9.I.80

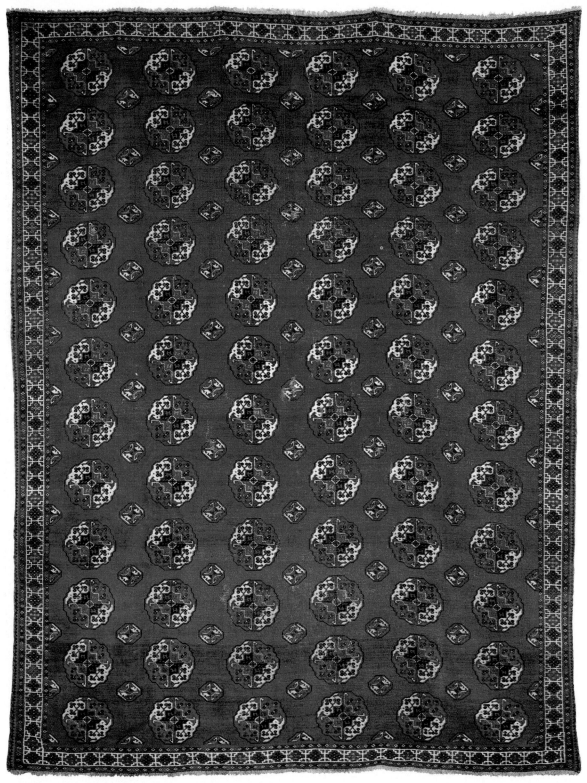

A Salor carpet, mid nineteenth century, 10ft 3in by 7ft 10in (312.5cm by 239cm)
PB Eighty-four $30,000 (£12,766). 19.III.80

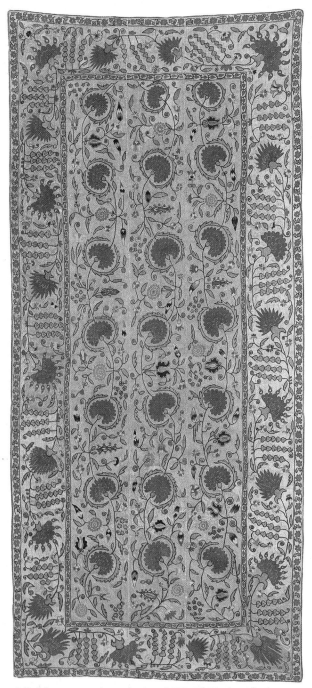

A Bokhara *susani* panel, *circa* 1870, 7ft 9in by 3ft 6in
(236cm by 107cm)
Zurich SFr 9,000 (£2,308:$5,423). 8.V.80

A Chinese carpet, early nineteenth century, 15ft 3in by 12ft 6in (465cm by 381cm)
New York $23,000 (£9,787). 8.III.80

A Chinese pillar rug, *circa* 1830, 10ft 1in by 4ft 3$\frac{1}{8}$in
(307cm by 130cm)
Hong Kong HK$36,000(£3,130:$7,357). 26.XI.79

A Navajo *serape*, 5ft 10½in by 4ft 2in (179cm by 127cm)
New York $16,000 (£6,809). 26.X.79

Antiquities, Asian and Primitive Art

A Mayan pottery figure of a priest, Jaina, Late Classic period, height 10⅜in (26.5cm)
New York $13,000 (£5,532). 10.V.80

Fig 1
A Benin bronze plaque of a warrior chief with retainers, *circa* 1600, height 19¼in (49cm)
London £180,000 ($423,000). 16.VI.80

The courtly art of Benin bronzes

Philip J.C. Dark

Archaeological evidence establishes that metals were being worked in West Africa in the fourth century BC. The artefacts of the Nok culture of central Nigeria show that West Africa advanced from an age of wood and stone tool manufacture to one of iron and then bronze, whereas the civilisations of the Middle East and the Mediterranean progressed through ages of copper and bronze before learning to work iron. The earliest evidence of bronze casting suggests that the technique was being practised in the ninth century AD. The well-known bronzes of Ife were made rather later, probably between the twelfth and fifteenth centuries. Benin bronze casting overlapped this period and may have first occurred in the thirteenth or fourteenth century, though, according to Connah, the bronzes which are archaeologically datable to that period – a number of manillas and bracelets – are not cast works but made by smithing. Interestingly, the tin bronze of these manillas and bracelets contrasts with the cast Benin bronzes, which are composed of zinc and copper – the calamine brass of European antiquity. Because the cast bronzes of Benin have other constituent elements in the ore besides zinc and copper, including lead and nickel, and arsenic and antimony, they could more accurately be termed brasses.

Bronze casting by the lost wax process varies considerably in West Africa with respect to the materials used in constructing the object, the manner of investing it to make a mould, the method of firing the clay protoform and the way in which the metal is poured into the mould, as well as to the composition of the ore used. The technique in Benin work, judging from the way it was still employed in the 1950s, seems to have been close to that used at Ife in twelfth- to fifteenth-century bronzes, and legend has it that Benin brass-smiths learned the art of casting from Ife. Bronze casting as carried out today at Benin differs from contemporary western techniques in that the elaborate system of gating and venting is not employed. Instead, the gases engendered by the molten metal at pouring are absorbed by a carboniferous clay investment, after passing through a fine clay slip, which preserves the detail of ornament and decoration chased in the wax original.

Metal is hard and unyielding, firm, static and structurally strong, the antitheses of soft and giving, yielding, dynamic and malleable; depending on context, of course, these qualities are either undesirable or desirable, and the latter prepares us for the threshold of aesthetic experience, while the former tends to repel. The bronze art of

Benin moves to stasis as it develops in time, losing flow and becoming increasingly unyielding, but its persistent imagery and the demands of its conventions continue. For example, the realistic head of an Oba (king) (Fig 2), in some places only 2mm thick, contrasts sharply with the heaviness of late nineteenth-century heads. For the Bini, the people of Benin, metal has supernatural qualities of strength and represents control of forces above the ordinary. Political position, regality, authority, and its ancestral sanction, are special and desirable qualities. Together with a recognition of the technical skill and supernatural control of the bronze-caster in being able to express them, these qualities form the basis of the Bini admiration for his art. This bronze work was a special form of aesthetic expression and was essentially a court art. The imagery is suited to the context for which the castings were intended; the appropriate qualities are expressed by the introduction of minor forms or such details of costume, weaponry and decorative features as those which elaborate the warrior chief with his retainers on a seventeenth-century plaque (Fig 1).

The number of different castings that survive is quite large, considering that many produced may have been melted down due to shortages of metal. Scholarly opinion is not unanimous as to the course of the development of Bini bronze casting, but it is convenient for the purpose of discussion to accept that the Bini learned the art of casting bronze during the reign of Oba Oguola, the sixth Oba of the present dynasty, that this occurred some time in the fourteenth century, and that it was the Ife bronze-smith, Igueghae, who taught the Bini the art. Of the twenty-one early memorial heads in existence, similar to Fig 2, it is uncertain whether any one of them was cast at that time, but it would seem that they are the first castings and the earliest to survive. Only one or two other items may have been made in this earliest period. Not until the arrival of the Portuguese, in 1485, and the reign of Oba Esigie in the first half of the sixteenth century, does the supply of brass become sufficient for a launching out into new forms. New styles of heads were produced, but perhaps the most striking forms were the plaques of which some nine hundred survive. They portray the courtly culture of the times, from the middle of the sixteenth into the first quarter of the seventeenth century. As well as picturing people, including kings and chiefs with their retainers and elaborate accoutrements (Fig 1), there are plaques of symbolic animals, scenes of the hunt and of war, plaques of Europeans, such as one of a splendid fowler, and plaques of individual items of regal costume, animals and decorative but symbolic forms – a veritable pictorial representation of Bini culture during the first 'golden' age of Benin art.

Established forms persisted, but with perhaps less fluidity of expression, until the second quarter of the eighteenth century during the reign of Oba Eresonye, a time of 'much brass'. New objects appeared, old ones continued with a change in expression, and attention was given to the formal aspects of decoration as a feature of form *per se* rather than as an adjunct to it. In the nineteenth century, when there was an increase in the number of memorial heads produced, an aridity of expression seemed to confine the Bini aesthetic more and more. With the hiatus caused by the British punitive expedition in 1897, and subsequent colonial rule, the corpus of original forms contracted and new ones were added in response to the demands which arose over and above the previous courtly focus of the bronze art.

Fig 2
A Benin bronze memorial head of an Oba, fourteenth century (?), height 8$\frac{7}{8}$in (22.5cm)
London £200,000 ($470,000). 16.VI.80

A Luba wood arrow rest figure, Zaire,
height 25¼in (64cm)
London £120,000 ($282,000). 16.VI.80
From the collection of Camila Pinto

A Benin ivory double bell, first half sixteenth
century, length 14⅛in (36cm)
London £130,000 ($305,500). 16.VI.80

A Mpongwe wood white-faced mask, Gabon, height 12¼in (31cm)
London £18,000 ($42,300). 16.VI.80
From the collection of Camila Pinto

A Tlingit wood clan hat, British Columbia, length 16in (40.5cm)
New York $34,000 (£14,468). 26.IV.80

A Yoruba wood double-faced Gelede mask, Nigeria, height 14in (35.5cm)
London £13,000 ($30,550). 16.VI.80
From the collection of Camila Pinto

A Pre-Columbian Chimu gold
beaker, *circa* 1000–1250 AD,
height 5¼in (13.5cm)
New York $15,500 (£6,596).
10.V.80
From the collection of the late
Mark Sheppard

A Sulka basketry helmet mask, New Britain, height 33in (84cm)
London £16,000 ($37,600). 16.VI.80

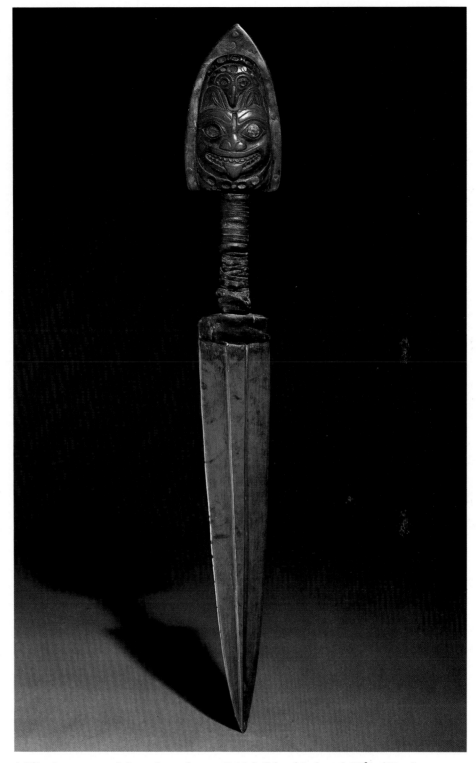

A Tlingit copper and sheep-horn dagger, British Columbia, length 22⅜in (57cm)
New York $72,000 (£30,638). 26.X.79

A Mayan painted pottery cylinder vase, Petán, Guatemala, Late Classic period, height 5¾in (14.5cm)
New York $31,000(£13,191). 10.V.80

An Iranian lustre pottery dish, Kashan, dated *AH 590* (1193 AD), diameter 21¼in (54cm)
London £12,000 ($28,200). 21.IV.80

A Japanese Vajradhatu mandala, gold and colour on silk, Muromachi period, 6ft 1½in by 4ft 3¾in (186.5cm by 131.5cm)
New York $9,000 (£3,830). 3.VII.80

A Gandhara grey schist figure of Buddha, third–fourth century AD, height 54in (137cm)
London £12,000 ($28,200). 23.VI.80

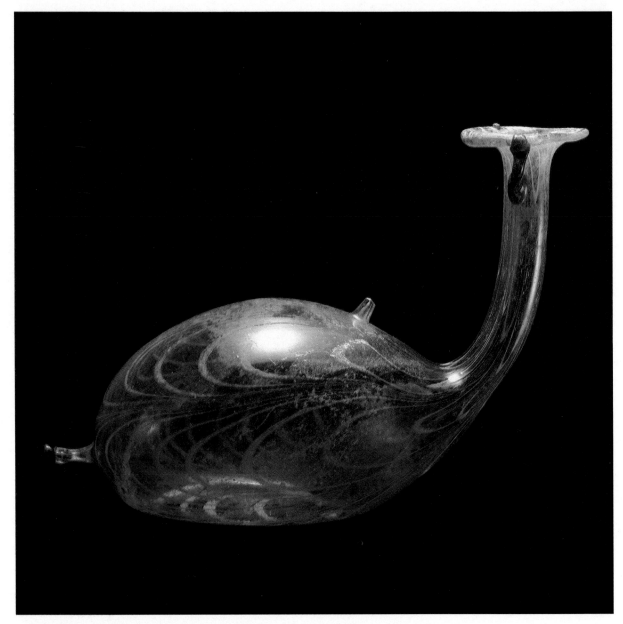

A Roman glass vessel in the form of a swan, Rhineland, late third–fourth century AD,
length 7⅝in (19.5cm)
New York $31,000(£13,191). 13.XII.79
From the collection of Richard Reedy

A Hellenistic millefiori glass bowl, late third–second century BC, diameter $5\frac{1}{4}$in (13.5cm)
New York $50,000 (£21,277). 13.XII.79
From the collection of Richard Reedy

An Assyrian gypsum relief of a divine figure, *circa* 883–859 BC, height 47in (119.5cm)
London £240,000 ($564,000). 4.XII.79

Sculptures from Sandon Hall

Richard Barnett

It is sobering to reflect that by the time our great grandfathers were born, the civilisations of Mesopotamia – the Sumerians, Assyrians and Babylonians – had perished so completely that scarcely a trace or even the knowledge of them remained. In 1842, however, a French excavator found an Assyrian palace at Khorsabad, near Mosul in northern Iraq. Between 1845 and 1851 the young Englishman, A. H. Layard, followed up that discovery and, supported by the Trustees of the British Museum, found and excavated near Mosul a series of palaces of the Assyrian kings of the ninth and eighth centuries BC. At Nimrud, Layard unearthed the palace of a mighty but hitherto unknown Assyrian king, Ashurnasirpal II (883–859 BC).

The walls of these royal residences were faced with stone slabs bearing long rows of splendid sculptures, in low relief: those at Nimrud showed great figures, royal and divine, scenes of ritual, court ceremonial and of war. There was then no Museum or Department of Antiquities in Turkey. The Trustees excavated until the outbreak of the Crimean War in 1854, and were authorised by the Sultan to take over all finds, including sculpture, made on their chosen sites. These 'heathen abominations', which embarrassed the Turkish government, aroused a frenzy of excitement in Europe and America, and the most important discoveries were displayed in the Crystal Palace Exhibition before being incorporated into the British Museum's collections.

In 1853 Lord Sandon, eldest son of Lord Harrowby, accompanied by Lord Carnarvon brought back to England two fine reliefs from the palace of Ashurnasirpal at Nimrud. One represents a four-winged, bearded divine figure (see opposite), facing right, richly dressed, wearing a divine head-dress with bull's horns, armed with knives and dagger, and holding what seems to be a pine cone. He is taking part in a rite, possibly of fertilisation of a symbolic 'tree of life'. In spite of the wealth of information recovered from the Assyrian cuneiform tablets this rite remains a mystery and the identity of the winged figure is still unknown. Across his waist on this slab is visible a part of a cuneiform inscription describing the military exploits and piety of King Ashurnasirpal in the service of his national god, Ashur, supreme god of the Assyrians. The sculpture is of the finest quality of the period, and comes from the palace's Room I, the walls of which were covered with a series of such slabs. The other piece represents a figure with a human body, but with four wings and an eagle's head. It is thought by some to be a masked priest but is more likely a deity, also performing the same ritual in the unseen world of magic. The room from which this piece came cannot now be certainly identified, but the line of cuneiform above the sculpture is part of the same text as that on the other slab.

An Egyptian lapis lazuli amulet in the form of a goddess, Ptolemaic period, height 2½in (6.3cm)
New York $19,000 (£8,085). 13.XII.79
From the collection of Edward M. Nagel

Two Egyptian red jasper inlays from the same figure, New Kingdom, height of head ¾in (2cm)
London £8,000 ($18,800). 15.VII.80

An Egyptian bronze figure of Anubis, Late period, length 8⅞in (22.5cm)
London £12,000 ($28,200). 15.VII.80
From the collection of D. Ramon

A Cycladic marble female figure, *circa* 2700–2500 BC, height 22½in (57cm)
London £32,000 ($75,200). 15.VII.80

An Egyptian bronze figure of Sekhmet, Late period, Twenty-sixth Dynasty,
height 10¾in (27.5cm)
London £15,500 ($36,425). 15.VII.80
From the collection of Camila Pinto

An Egyptian black basalt head of a king, Ptolemaic period, *circa* 250–150 BC,
height 10¼in (26cm)
New York $28,000 (£11,915). 16.V.80

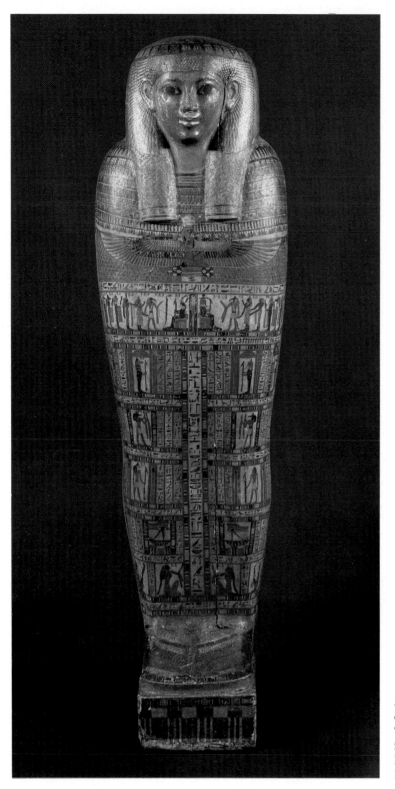

An Egyptian painted wood anthropoid
coffin for the Lady of the House Taawa,
Thebes, Late period, Twenty-
fifth–Twenty-sixth Dynasty,
height 68½in (174cm)
London £17,000 ($39,950). 15.VII.80

Chinese Paintings, Ceramics and Works of Art

River landscape
Album leaf, ink and colour on silk, two character mark of Xia Shen,
thirteenth–fifteenth century, 10in by 10in (25.5cm by 25.5cm)
New York $10,000 (£4,255). 17.VI.80
From the collection of the late Stevenson Burke

FU BAOSHI
Lady Xiang and falling leaves
Hanging scroll, ink and colour on
paper, four seals of the artist, 1960,
inscribed with a dedication
dated *1962*, 39in by 21¼in
(99cm by 54cm)
Hong Kong HK $180,000
(£15,652 : $36,783). 28.V.80

WEN ZHENG MING
Master Liu's garden (living aloft)
Hanging scroll, ink and colour on paper,
signed and with four seals of the artist,
inscribed with a poem by the artist and
dated *1543*, 37½in by 18in (95cm by 45.5cm)
New York $110,000 (£46,809). 2.XI.79

A three-colour-glazed pottery figure of a foreign merchant with a goose, Tang Dynasty,
height 12½in (32cm)
New York $91,000 (£38,723). 2.XI.79

A painted pottery figure of a foreign dancer, Tang Dynasty,
height 10½in (26.5cm)
New York $33,000 (£14,043). 2.XI.79

A glazed pottery Cizhou pillow in the form of a lady,
Jin Dynasty, length 16¾in (42.5cm)
London £23,000 ($54,050). 15.IV.80

An Imperial Ruyao brushwasher, Northern Song Dynasty, diameter $5\frac{1}{4}$in (13.5cm)
London £105,000 ($246,750). 15.IV.80

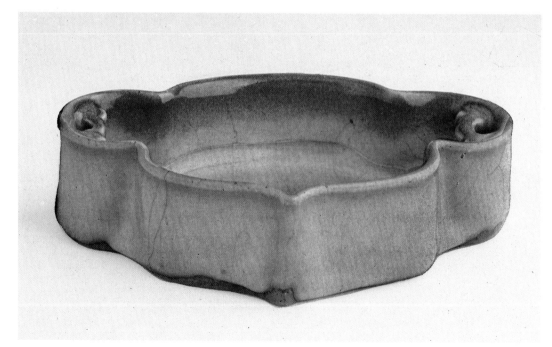

A Junyao quatrefoil (*ruyi*) washer, Song Dynasty, width 5in (12.5cm)
London £27,000 ($63,450). 15.VII.80
From the collection of W. W. Winkworth

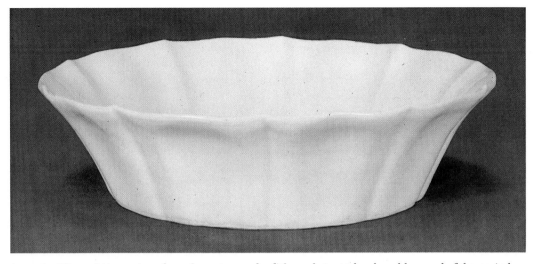

An early Ming white washer, four character mark of Zhengde in underglaze-blue, and of the period, diameter 7⅝in (19.5cm)
Hong Kong HK$340,000 (£29,565 : $69,478). 20.V.80

An early Ming red-glazed stemcup, four character mark of Yongle, and of the period, height 4¼in (11cm)
London £55,000 ($129,250). 15.IV.80

A Ming blue and white stemcup, period of Chenghua, height $4\frac{1}{2}$in (11.5cm)
London £40,000 ($94,000). 11.XII.79

A blue and white vase, dated *1636*,
Transitional period, height
$9\frac{1}{4}$in (23.5cm)
London £12,500 ($29,375). 11.XII.79

A blue and white *guan*, mid fourteenth century, height 11in (28cm)
London £132,000 ($310,200). 15.IV.80

Two views of a blue and white palace bowl, six character mark of Chenghua, and of the period, diameter 5¾in (14.5cm)
Hong Kong HK$1,800,000 (£156,522: $367,826). 20.V.80
From the collection of the late Lord Cunliffe

A blue and white *guan*, six character mark of Chenghua, and of the period, height $4\frac{1}{8}$in (10.5cm)
London £265,000 ($622,750). 15.VII.80

Two views of a Ming *doucai* dish, six character mark of Jiajing, and of the period,
diameter 5¾in (14.5cm)
Hong Kong HK $260,000 (£22,609 : $53,130). 28.XI.79

A Ming green dragon bowl, six character mark of Zhengde, and of the period,
diameter 7¼in (18.5cm)
London £42,000 ($98,700). 15.IV.80
From the collection of the late Lord Cunliffe

A *famille rose* flask, seal mark of Qianlong in underglaze-blue, and of the period, height 9in (23cm)
Hong Kong HK $500,000 (£43,478 : $102,174). 28.XI.79

A pair of *famille rose* pheasants, period of Qianlong, height 15¾in (40cm)
Monte Carlo FF 190,000 (£19,588 : $46,031). 27.V.80

A pair of biscuit equestrian figures, period of Kangxi, height $8\frac{1}{4}$in (21cm)
Monte Carlo FF 110,000 (£11,340 : $26,649). 27.V.80

A Chinese export documentary charger, painted with the Dutch East Indiaman *Vrÿburg*, inscribed and dated *1756*, diameter 14in (35.5cm)
Pokety Farms $16,000 (£6,809). 22.V.80
From the collection of the late Bernice Chrysler Garbisch

An interior-painted glass snuff
bottle with a portrait of Kaiser
Wilhelm II by Ma Shaoxuan,
dated *1910*, height 2⅛in (5.5cm)
PB Eighty-four
$20,000(£8,511). 11.X.79
From the collection of the late
Dr and Mrs Louis E. Wolferz

A Peking enamel snuff
bottle, four character mark,
Kangxi yuzhi, and of the
period of Kangxi,
height 2in (5cm)
London £4,000 ($9,400).
18.III.80

An enamelled milk-glass
snuff bottle, four character
mark of Qianlong, and of the
period, height 2⅞in (7.2cm)
PB Eighty-four
$50,000(£21,277). 11.X.79
From the collection of
Dr Sidney A. Levine

A Peking enamel snuff bottle
decorated with European
figures, four character mark of
Qianlong, and of the period,
height 2in (5cm)
London £10,500 ($24,675).
18.III.80

A *cloisonné* Dog-of-Fo, period of Qianlong, height $18\frac{7}{8}$in (48cm)
London £14,250($33,488). 7.III.80

A hardwood group of a *lohan* seated on a lion, Qianlong mark and period, height 3¾in (9.5cm)
New York $6,750 (£2,872). 28.II.80

An archaic bronze aquamanile, Six Dynasties, length 5⅝in (14.5cm)
New York $19,000 (£8,085). 2.XI.79

An archaic jade columnar bead,
late Western Zhou Dynasty,
length 2⅝in (6.7cm)
New York $42,000 (£17,872). 2.XI.79
From the collection of the late
Charlotte B. McKim

An archaic jade pendant in the form
of a bird, Shang Dynasty,
length 2⅞in (7.2cm)
New York $17,000 (£7,234). 2.XI.79
From the collection of the late
Charlotte B. McKim

A jade figure of a chimera, Six Dynasties, length 3¼in (8.3cm)
New York $23,000 (£9,787). 2.XI.79

A jadeite hanging vase, height 10⅝in (27cm)
Hong Kong HK $330,000 (£28,696 : $67,435). 29.XI.79

A jadeite figure of Guanyin the Maternal,
height 10⅝in (27cm)
Hong Kong HK $520,000 (£45,217 : $106,261). 29.XI.79

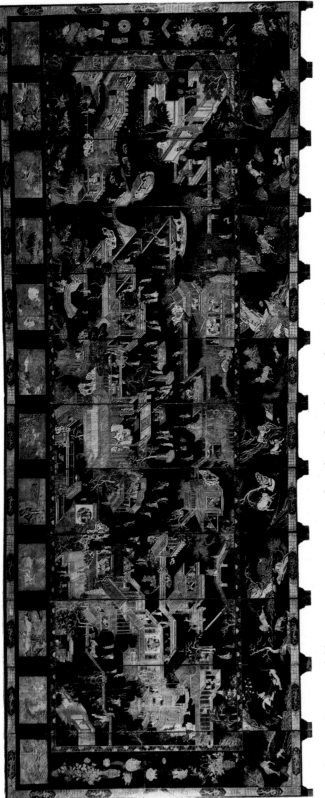

A twelve-panel Coromandel lacquer screen, *circa* 1670, 10ft 3in by 25ft 3in (312.5cm by 770cm)
Los Angeles $145,000 (£61,702). 5.VI.80
From the collection of the late Violet Rosenberg

Two of a set of four *kesi* panels,
eighteenth century, 4ft $\frac{3}{8}$in by
2ft 1$\frac{3}{4}$in (123cm by 65.5cm)
London £4,200 ($9,870). 7.III.80

A *huang huali* table, early Ming Dynasty, height 1ft $\frac{1}{4}$in (31cm)
New York $27,000 (£11,489). 8.V.80

An Imperial yellow Pekin glass vase, seal mark of
Qianlong, height 8½in (21.5cm)
New York $10,000(£4,255). 28.II.80

A Peking enamel censer, four character mark, Kangxi yuzhi, and of the period of Kangxi,
diameter 4¼in (11cm)
Hong Kong HK $135,000(£11,739:$27,587). 21.V.80

Japanese Prints, Ceramics and Works of Art

A gold lacquer *shodana*, Meiji period, height 2ft 7¾in (80.5cm)
New York $25,000 (£10,638). 13.XII.79

HOKUSAI KATSUSHIKA
South wind and clear weather
Oban, signed, *circa* 1820–30
New York $43,000 (£18,298). 2.VII.80

SUZUKI HARUNOBU
A young man seated before a 'tokonoma' playing a 'ko-tsuzumi'
Chuban, unsigned, mid eighteenth century
New York $10,000 (£4,255). 20.XI.79

A silver lacquer *inro* by Koma
Kansai, signed, nineteenth
century
£11,500($27,025)

A green lacquer *inro* by Koma
Kansai, signed, nineteenth
century
£9,500($22,325)

An *inro* with pale grey ground by Shibata
Zeshin, signed, nineteenth century
£8,500($19,975)

The *inro* on this page were sold in London on 29 May 1980

A wood study of a boar by
Toyomasa II, signed, Tamba,
early nineteenth century
Los Angeles $20,000 (£8,511).
6.III.80

A wood study of a boar by
Ichimin, signed, Nagoya,
nineteenth century
New York $5,750 (£2,447).
13.XII.79

A wood group of two rats
by Ikkan, signed,
Nagoya, nineteenth
century
London £5,800 ($13,630).
29.V.80

A wood figure of a Chinese musician,
unsigned, eighteenth century
London £5,500 ($12,925). 29.V.80

A wood group of Ashinaga and Tenaga
by Masatoshi, signed, nineteenth
century
London £4,200 ($9,870). 29.V.80

An ivory study of a tiger by
Tomotada, signed, Kyoto,
eighteenth century
£6,000 ($14,100)

An ivory figure of Gama
Sennin by Tomotada,
signed, Kyoto, eighteenth
century
£7,000 ($16,450)

An ivory group of a cow and calf by
Tomotada, signed, Kyoto,
eighteenth century
£2,500 ($5,875)

An ivory study of a stallion
by Okatomo, signed, Kyoto,
eighteenth century
£25,000 ($58,750)

An ivory study of a turtle by
Seiyodo Bunshojo, signed, Iwami,
early nineteenth century
£6,200 ($14,570)

The *netsuke* on this page were sold in London on 29 May 1980

Left An ivory figure of a farmer by Hirasaka Hobun, signed, Tokyo, *circa* 1900,
height 13⅜in (34cm)
£2,100 ($4,935)
Right An ivory group of a poulterer and his son by Kyosai, signed, Tokyo,
circa 1900, height 13⅜in (34cm)
£2,800 ($6,580)

The figures on this page were sold at Belgravia on 14 April 1980

A lacquer wood *tate-byobu*, Meiji period, height 7ft 3¾in (223cm)
Los Angeles $21,000 (£8,936). 6.III.80

A parcel-gilt bronze group of a Samurai warrior and two *oni* by Miyao, signed, late nineteenth century, height 21¾in (55cm)
Belgravia £6,200 ($14,570). 14.II.80

Two views of a vase by Yabu Meizan, signed, late nineteenth century, height 12⅜in (31.5cm) Belgravia £2,500 ($5,875). 8.V.80

A Kakiemon dish, late seventeenth
century, diameter 9¼in (23.5cm)
London £6,200 ($14,570). 5.VI.80

A Kakiemon dish, third quarter seventeenth
century, diameter 12⅝in (32cm)
London £3,500 ($8,225). 7.XI.79
From the collection of Richard de la Mare

A Kakiemon figure of a young boy seated on a *go* table, late seventeenth century, height 8¼in (21cm)
London £7,000 ($16,450). 7.XI.79

European Ceramics

A Lowestoft blue and white bottle, painted by Richard Phillips, inscribed in underglaze-blue
E·A Lowestoft and dated *1764*, height 9½in (24cm)
Pokety Farms $15,000 (£6,383). 22.V.80
From the collection of the late Bernice Chrysler Garbisch

A pair of Worcester soup plates and a plate, from the Duke of Gloucester service, painted by the
'Spotted Fruit Painter', first period, *circa* 1775, diameter of each $8\frac{7}{8}$in (22.5cm)
New York $21,000 (£8,936); $11,000 (£4,681). 15.IV.80
From the collection of the late Donald S. Morrison

A Worcester yellow-scale teapot and cover, painted in the manner of James Giles, first period,
1765–70, height 6½in (16.5cm)
New York $22,000 (£9,362). 11.IV.80
From the collection of the late Nelson A. Rockefeller

A Chelsea figure of a Jewish pedlar, marked with red anchor, *circa* 1752–56, height 7¼in (18.5cm)
London £4,000 ($9,400). 20.V.80
From the collection of Sir Henry and Lady Tate

A Chelsea pigeon tureen and cover, marked with red anchor, *circa* 1755, length 8½in (21.5cm)
New York $29,000 (£12,340). 11.IV.80
From the collection of the late Nelson A. Rockefeller

A Ralph Wood model of a stag, *circa* 1770, height 13½in (34.5cm)
New York $17,000 (£7,234). 11.IV.80
From the collection of the late Nelson A. Rockefeller

A Ralph Wood figure of Benjamin Franklin, *circa* 1775, height 13¼in (33.5cm)
New York $12,500 (£5,319). 11.IV.80
From the collection of the late Nelson A. Rockefeller

A 'blue-dash' tulip charger, possibly Bristol, *circa* 1660–80,
diameter 16in (40.5cm)
£4,800 ($11,280)
From the collection of the late Sir Geoffrey Selby Church

Left A 'blue-dash' tulip charger, London, *circa* 1680,
diameter 13¼in (33.5cm)
£2,200 ($5,170)
Right A 'blue-dash' charger, London, *circa* 1780,
diameter 12½in (31.5cm)
£2,200 ($5,170)
Both from the collection of Marion Morgan and Brian Morgan

The pottery on this page was sold in London on 25 March 1980

A Meissen figure of an eagle, modelled by Johann Gottlob Kirchner, *circa* 1731, height 20in (51cm)
New York $42,500 (£18,085). 11.IV.80
From the collection of the late Nelson A. Rockefeller

A pair of Meissen hoopoes, modelled by Johann Joachim Kaendler or Johann Gottlieb Ehder, 1736–45, height 12¼in (31cm)
Monte Carlo FF 130,000 (£13,402 : $31,495). 26.V.80

A Hausmaler Meissen milk jug and cover, decorated at Augsburg with silver-gilt mounts by Elias
Adam, the porcelain *circa* 1720, the decoration *circa* 1730, height $7\frac{5}{8}$in (19.5cm)
Monte Carlo FF 240,000 (£24,742 : $58,144). 26.V.80

A Meissen pagoda figure, 1720–25,
height $3\frac{7}{8}$in (10cm)
London £10,000 ($23,500). 27.XI.79

A Meissen teapot and cover, painted by Johann Gregor Höroldt and with silver-gilt mounts by Elias
Adam of Augsburg, inscribed *KPM* and marked with crossed swords in underglaze-blue, *circa* 1723,
height $4\frac{3}{4}$in (12cm)
London £9,500 ($22,325). 27.XI.79

A Sèvres tray, painted by Louis-Bertin Parant, signed and dated *1817*,
height 20⅛in (51cm)
London £5,400($12,690). 16.X.79

A Strasbourg faience polychrome pheasant tureen and cover, Paul Hannong period, *circa* 1760,
length 28½in (72.5cm)
New York $40,000 (£17,021). 17.V.80
From the collection of the late Bernice Chrysler Garbisch

Left One of a pair of Dutch Delft polychrome plaques, inscribed *JB*, eighteenth century,
height 9⅞in (25cm)
London £2,400 ($5,640). 1.VII.80
Right A Dutch Delft polychrome plaque, eighteenth century, height 9⅞in (25cm)
London £1,000 ($2,350). 1.VII.80

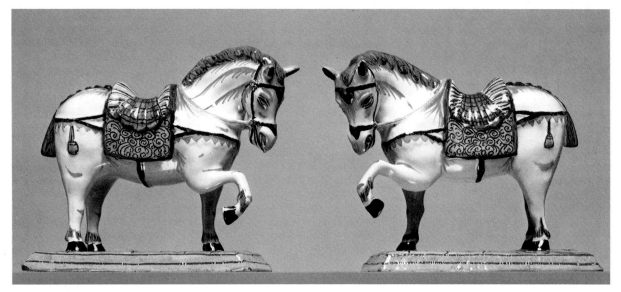

A pair of Dutch Delft polychrome horses, inscribed *P:V:M*, 1759–64, length of each
8½in (21.5cm); 8¾in (22cm)
Pokety Farms $28,000 (£11,915). 22.V.80
From the collection of the late Bernice Chrysler Garbisch

A Florentine 'oak leaf' jar, first half fifteenth century, height 9⅝in (24.5cm)
London £25,000 ($58,750). 11.III.80

An Urbino Gubbio-lustred *istoriato* dish, painted by Francesco Xanto Avelli, *circa* 1535,
diameter 10½in (26.5cm)
New York $29,000 (£12,340). 31.V.80

A 'Sèvres' gilt-bronze-mounted earthenware vase and cover,
late nineteenth century, height 54in (137cm)
Los Angeles $16,500 (£7,021). 3.VI.80

A Berlin plaque, painted by M. Beetz after Rubens, late nineteenth century, height 15$\frac{1}{2}$in (39.5cm)
PB Eighty-four $21,000 (£8,936). 24.X.79

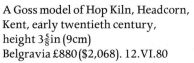

A Goss model of Hop Kiln, Headcorn, Kent, early twentieth century, height $3\frac{5}{8}$in (9cm)
Belgravia £880 ($2,068). 12.VI.80

A Mintons 'Majolica' teapot and cover, after a model by John Henk, 1874, height $5\frac{3}{4}$in (14.5cm)
Belgravia £110 ($259). 13.IX.79

A Royal Worcester pierced box and cover by George Owen, 1909, length $6\frac{1}{4}$in (16cm)
Belgravia £1,400 ($3,290). 27.XI.79

A Royal Doulton 'Sung' vase by Arthur Eaton and Cecil J. Noke, 1923,
height $15\frac{3}{4}$in (40cm)
Belgravia £2,100 ($4,935). 6.XII.79

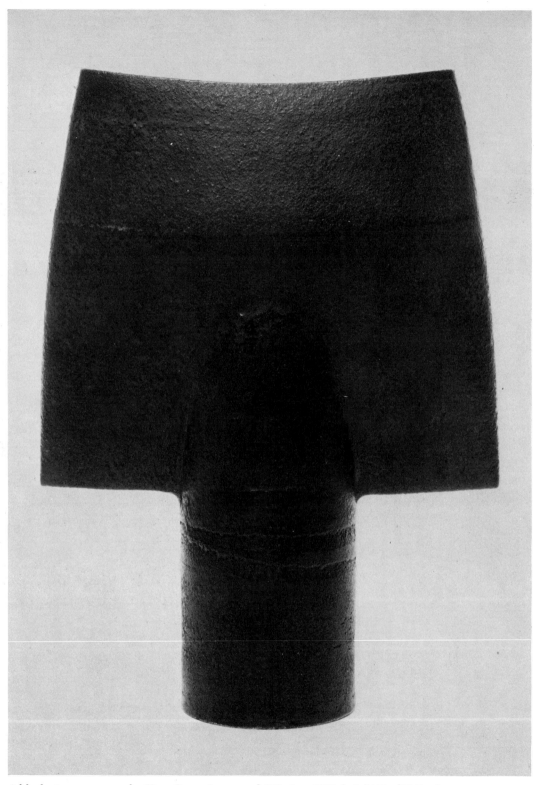

A black stoneware vase by Hans Coper, impressed *HC*, *circa* 1970, height 8in (20.5cm)
Belgravia £1,050 ($2,468). 6.XII.79

Silver and Pewter

A set of four candlesticks from the Orloff service, maker's mark of Jacques-Nicolas Roettiers, Paris, 1771–72, height 12⅝in (32cm)
Zurich SFr 480,000 (£123,077:$289,231). 7.V.80

One of a set of four candelabra, maker's mark of Robert-Joseph Auguste, Paris, 1779–81,
height 22in (56cm)
Monte Carlo FF1,300,000 (£134,021:$314,948). 27.XI.79
From the collection of Claude Cartier

One of a pair of soup tureens with covers and stands, maker's mark of Robert-Joseph Auguste, Paris,
1778–80, width of tureen 16½in (42cm)
Monte Carlo FF950,000 (£97,938:$230,155). 27.XI.79
From the collection of Claude Cartier

Left and right A pair of silver-gilt candlesticks, maker's mark of Tilman Wendel(s), Cologne, *circa* 1720, height $7\frac{7}{8}$in (20cm)
SFr 22,000 (£5,641:$13,256)
Centre One of a set of twenty-six silver-gilt dinner plates, engraved with the arms of Frederick Augustus I, Elector of Saxony and King of Poland, maker's mark of Christian Winter or Christoph Warmberger, Augsburg, *circa* 1730, diameter $9\frac{5}{8}$in (24.5cm)
SFr 510,000 (£130,769:$307,308)

The silver on this page was sold in Zurich on 7 May 1980

A silver-gilt and coral stag and hunting dog, maker's mark of Meinrad Bauch the Elder, Nuremberg,
circa 1600, height 14⅝in (37cm)
Monte Carlo FF 1,000,000 (£103,093 : $242,268). 27.XI.79

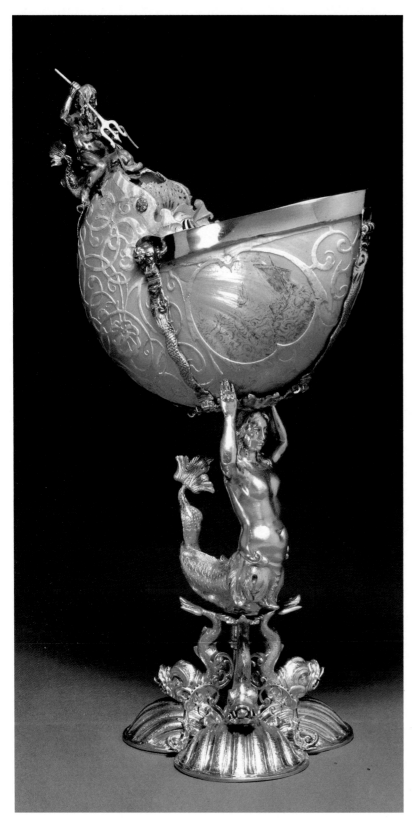

A Dutch silver-gilt nautilus cup,
maker's mark possibly of the Master
of the Scissors, Vlissingen, 1627,
height 14½in (37cm)
New York $56,000 (£23,830).
17.IV.80

A George IV silver-gilt dressing set in a brass-bound mahogany case, maker's mark of Mary & Charles
Reily, London, 1828, width of largest box 7¾in (19.5cm)
Lennoxlove £13,000 ($30,550). 24.VI.80
From the collection of the Duke of Hamilton and Brandon

A communion cup, maker's mark of
William Lindsay II, Montrose, *circa* 1688,
height 8in (20.5cm)
London £8,000 ($18,800). 12.VI.80

An American coffee pot, maker's mark of Paul Revere Jr,
Boston, *circa* 1775, height 12¼in (31cm)
New York $64,000 (£27,234). 30.IV.80

Two of six George III silver-gilt
coasters, maker's mark of Paul
Storr, London, 1814, diameter
5¾in (14.5cm)
London £24,000 ($56,400).
12.VI.80

A George II salver, maker's mark of Paul de Lamerie, London, 1743, diameter 22in (56cm)
New York $122,500 (£52,128). 6.VI.80
From the collection of the late Donald S. Morrison

Fig 1
A George II seal salver, engraved with the Exchequer seal of George I by Samuel Gribelin, maker's mark of Edward Vincent, London, 1728, diameter 13½in (34.5cm)

The seal salvers on these pages are from the collection of the late Donald S. Morrison and were sold as one lot in New York on 6 June 1980 for $180,000 (£76,596)

The seal salvers of
Lord Chief Justice Robert Eyre

John Hayward

Until the early nineteenth century, ambassadors and senior officers of state were allowed to retain as a perquisite the royal plate issued by the Jewel Office to enable them to maintain a degree of state appropriate to their office. This custom has resulted in considerable numbers of vessels of precious metal, bearing the royal arms, passing to other hands. A much rarer perquisite of office was the silver from the matrices of the various seals of state. Since the seventeenth century, it has been customary in England for the holder of an office, which entitled him to a seal, to retain the silver matrix when the seal became obsolete. This happened when the Sovereign died or a change in his title necessitated an alteration in the wording. The seal matrix was then broken or otherwise defaced, and the precious metal returned to the holder of the office. Since the early seventeenth century, the recipient of the silver sometimes commissioned a cup engraved with a representation of the seal from the matrix of which it was made.

During the reign of William III, it became the custom to have a salver made, the top of which was engraved with both sides of the seal, while the remaining area was engraved with the royal arms and those of the officer who had used the seal, within a surround of mantling or of foliate scrollwork. Among the few late seventeenth- or early eighteenth-century salvers, which have fortunately escaped the melting pot, the rarest and the most interesting are these seal salvers. The earliest known was made from the seal of Charles Montagu, Earl of Halifax, as Chancellor of the Exchequer. It required renewal in 1694 as a result of the death of William III's consort, Mary Stuart. It survives in the Burrell Collection, Glasgow, and is distinguished by its superb engraved ornament. In the seventeenth century the salver had been a piece of useful plate and had served to support a cup or bowl, when it was offered to a guest. The splendid engraving on these seal salvers was not, however, intended to be obscured by the base of a cup; the seal salver was a piece of display plate. This is proved by the untouched condition of those that survive.

The two salvers from the collection of the late Donald S. Morrison bear the London hallmarks for 1728 (Fig 1) and 1735 (Fig 2); they are engraved with representations of two seals rendered obsolete by the death of George I in 1727. These had been held by Sir Robert Eyre, in respect of his offices as Chief Baron of the Exchequer and

Chancellor of the Principality of Wales. The difference in date is curious. The delay can perhaps be explained by cost, as, in addition to the charge for workmanship, it was necessary to add extra silver in order to make a salver. An alternative explanation is that the decision to engrave both salvers was not taken until 1735 or 1736, the year of Sir Robert's death. This would imply that the silver used for the earlier salver did not necessarily come from the disused Exchequer seal.

Born in 1666, Sir Robert Eyre had an eminently successful legal career. He was called to the Bar in 1689, was elected to Parliament in 1698 and appointed Solicitor-General in 1708. He resigned from this post in 1710 and was appointed a judge. On the death of Queen Anne his support of the Hanoverian succession led to his appointment as Chancellor of the Principality of Wales. With this office went a special patent which entitled him, in spite of his position as a judge, to advise the Prince of Wales and receive fees for so doing. In the year following his appointment he took a risk by supporting the Prince of Wales, in a difference with his father George I, concerning the former's marriage. This did not work to his disadvantage, for in 1722 he was appointed Lord Chief Baron of the Exchequer and in 1725 Chief Justice of the Common Pleas. He died in 1736, having numbered among his friends prominent figures of his time, including Godolphin, Walpole and the Duke of Marlborough.

Edward Vincent, the goldsmith who made the first salver in 1728, was a craftsman of considerable repute. He is thought to have been apprenticed in 1699 to Robert Cooper and admitted as a Freeman of the Goldsmiths' Company in 1712. He was a maker of hollow ware, that is, coffee pots, cups and salvers. The second salver is perhaps the work of John Liger, son of the better-known Huguenot goldsmith, Isaac Liger. Little is known about him, but he followed his father in supplying plate to that great patron of Huguenot goldsmiths, the second Earl of Warrington.

The most skilled engraver of silver of the early decades of the eighteenth century was the Huguenot artist, Simon Gribelin, who came to England before 1686. He was commissioned to engrave the seal salver of Lord Halifax, as well as several others which have not survived. The chance preservation of a book, in which he entered proofs and counter-proofs of his engravings, has given us an idea of the range and character of his work. It was Gribelin who engraved the next two salvers made from Exchequer seals: that rendered obsolete on the death of William III in 1702 and also that discarded in 1707 after the union with Scotland, which necessitated alteration of the wording. Both are at Chatsworth in the collection of the Duke of Devonshire.

The design of the two Eyre salvers corresponds precisely with that of the two salvers at Chatsworth and their engraving can be attributed to Simon Gribelin's son, Samuel. The two salvers seem to have been engraved by the same hand: this could not have been Simon who died in 1733. Samuel was apprenticed to two Huguenot goldsmiths in succession and subsequently assisted his father. According to Horace Walpole the 'son graved in his father's manner', but whereas the latter had considerable success, the son eventually sought another occupation and left England in the retinue of the Earl of Kinnoul 'to draw prospects'.

Fig 2
A George II seal salver, engraved with the seal of the Prince of Wales by Samuel Gribelin, maker's mark I.L., attributed to John Liger, London, 1735, diameter $13\frac{1}{2}$in (34.5cm)

A royal presentation silver-gilt cup and cover, maker's mark of Paul Storr of Storr & Mortimer,
London, 1837, height 14in (35.5cm)
New York $37,000 (£15,745). 10.VI.80

The Doncaster Cup, maker's mark of John S. Hunt of Hunt & Roskell, London, 1852,
height of group 25¼in (64cm)
Toronto Can$34,000 (£12,593:$29,593). 16.IV.80

This group after Alfred Brown depicts a scene from the Battle of Flodden, September 1513

A parcel-gilt pilgrim flask, maker's mark of Charles T. and George Fox, London, 1850, height 26in (66cm)
Los Angeles $10,000 (£4,255). 7.XI.79

This flask was exhibited by the retail goldsmiths, Lambert & Rawlings of Coventry Street, Leicester Square, at the Great Exhibition of 1851; a companion flask from the same exhibition is in the Victoria and Albert Museum

A pair of Viennese silver-gilt-mounted enamel double-headed ostrich cups and covers, late nineteenth century, height $20\frac{3}{8}$in (51.5cm)
Belgravia £23,000($54,050). 13.XII.79

A vinaigrette with a view of the New Royal
Exchange, maker's mark of Frederick Marson,
Birmingham, 1844, width 2in (5.2cm)
Belgravia £670 ($1,575). 13.XII.79

A model of a long-eared owl, maker's mark of C. F.
Hancock's & Co, London, 1871, height 19¼in (49cm)
Belgravia £3,900 ($9,165). 8.V.80

A water jug in the form of a satyr, maker's mark of
Alexander Macrae, London, 1859, height 9¼in (23.5cm)
Belgravia £3,200 ($7,520). 6.III.80

A James I relief-cast wine cup, inscribed in eight rectangular panels around the bowl *THOUGH WINE BEE GOOD TOO MUCH OF THAT WIL MAKE ONE LEAN THOUGH HE BE FATT*, circa 1616, height 5$\frac{7}{8}$in (15cm)
London £4,200 ($9,870). 28.III.80

An American flat-top tankard, maker's mark of Henry Will, New York, *circa* 1770, height 7$\frac{1}{8}$in (18cm)
New York $8,250 (£3,511). 28.XI.79
From the collection of the late Charles M. Talley

Left A Stuart lidless tavern pot, late seventeenth century, height 5$\frac{7}{8}$in (15cm)
London £1,700 ($3,995). 28.III.80
Right One of a set of six Charles II broad-rimmed plates, maker's mark of William Matthews, London, *circa* 1675, diameter 9$\frac{3}{8}$in (24cm)
London £1,600 ($3,760). 28.III.80

Veteran and Vintage Vehicles

An 1893/94 Panhard et Levassor 'Paris-Rouen' type Dogcart
Kenilworth £25,000 ($58,750). 27.VIII.79

This car was sold totally unrestored

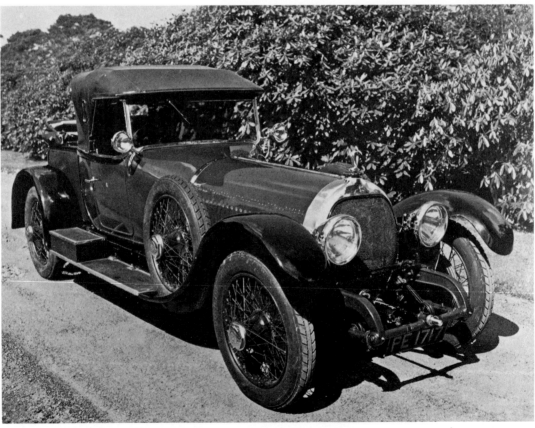

A 1920 Sheffield-Simplex 48hp Double Victoria by Cunard
Kenilworth £33,000 ($77,550). 27.VIII.79

A B.A.T. 492 cc solo motorcycle, *circa* 1902
Donington £2,000 ($4,700). 19.IV.80

This motorcycle was last used in 1912 and was sold totally unrestored

A 1914 Rolls-Royce Silver Ghost 'Alpine Eagle' replica tourer
Kenilworth £31,500 ($74,025). 27.VIII.79

From left to right
Orange Curaçao, early nineteenth
century (one bottle)
London £49 ($115). 26.IX.79
From the cellars of the Duke of
Northumberland

Cognac Bisquit Dubouché, Grande
Fine Champagne, 1811 (one bottle)
London £340 ($799). 12.XII.79

Malvazia 1790 (one bottle)
London £150 ($353). 26.IX.79

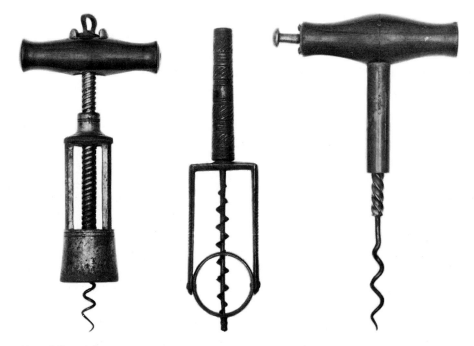

From left to right
A G. Twigg 1867 patent corkscrew; London £320 ($752). 12.XII.79
A French iron pocket corkscrew, *circa* 1760; London £1,070 ($2,515). 12.XII.79
A C. Hull patent presto corkscrew; London £310 ($729). 12.XII.79

Wine

It is ten years since the Wine Department was formed at Sotheby's. With the exception of a catalogue produced in 1868 devoted entirely to the sale of 1,300 dozens of Rhine wines, at Sotheby's Wellington Street, Strand, sales of wine were held as part of general house sales and only infrequently. Since the season of 1970–71, annual net sales have risen steadily to the present total of £1,344,196($3,158,861). Although there has been some levelling off in the price of the majority of finer wines, reflecting the international reduction in consumer demand and high interest rates, wine consumption overall continues to expand.

There have been eighteen sales in London, one near Edinburgh, one each in Pulborough and Taunton, and one in Amsterdam. For the sixth year running, Sotheby's conducted the annual auction of rare Cape wines at Nederburg on behalf of Stellenbosch Farmers' Wineries, which totalled £240,200($564,470).

In this last season nearly 13,500 lots were catalogued, compared with 3,337 at the beginning of the last decade, giving some indication of the growing importance of the wine auctions as a part of the general market. Nearly all wines that are available from traditional merchants are of the younger vintages, for laying-down; it is only in the salerooms that the maturer wines can be found. Many vendors are private owners who, in these inflationary times, see an opportunity of disposing of part of their reserve at a reasonable profit. Undoubtedly, there are still magnificent cellars lying undisturbed and sometimes forgotten, and a few of these come to light each season.

Fine and rare wines from some exceptional private cellars in Belgium, France, Germany, Holland, Italy, Sweden and Switzerland have appeared in the salerooms. Private reserves from the cellars at Châteaux Batailley and Cantemerle were included in a sale in May, and, in June, an entire morning was devoted to a sale of wines from over sixty California wineries.

Among some of the more interesting wines sold this season were a dozen bottles Château Cheval Blanc 1947, £1,350($3,173); a jeroboam Château Climens 1921, £500 ($1,175); a dozen bottles Romanée Conti 1971, £820($1,927); a magnum Cockburn 1927, £86($202). Some particularly fine corkscrews, wine books and related items have been included in the sales. A late George II mahogany bottle carrier sold for £720($1,692); a copy of Vizetelly's *History of Champagne* (1882) reached £125 ($294) and an exceptional price of £1,070($2,515) was achieved for a French iron pocket corkscrew, *circa* 1760. Nineteenth-century corkscrews, mechanically fine examples of an age of great craftsmanship, can still be collected for a modest outlay.

A tribute to A. J. B. Kiddell

Frank Herrmann

During the three years I shared Jim Kiddell's office, I relived with him every phase of his long life from his childhood in India, his momentous wartime experiences in France between 1914 and 1918, up to his arrival in Bond Street as Works Manager after a series of memorable interviews with Sir Montague Barlow and his partners. Jim's primary responsibility was to breathe new vigour into the organisation, to supervise the porters, to improve administration as well as the maintenance of the premises, but within a few months of his arrival he was taking the Friday sales, and soon he began to catalogue.

While researching Sotheby's past, I came across a long report which Geoffrey Hobson had prepared in 1945, on what the firm had achieved between 1939 and the return of peace. Jim, who became a director in 1949, had never seen it before.

> The success of our works of art department is largely due to Mr. Kiddell, by far the best expert in that field we have ever had. He is ready to catalogue everything in this department except silver and jewellery. He is our only cataloguer of rugs, which have recently become important – probably in 1942/43 the turnover in rugs and carpets alone was not far from the total of pictures and drawings. He has a great reputation in the art world as an expert on ceramics generally and is particularly good on early Chinese art; the Eumorfopoulos Collection came to us through him and that helped to bring various other sales – Bernet, Norman Collie, Daniel Hall and Lionel Edwards – to name only a few. He has a first rate knowledge of glass and miniatures and a more than adequate knowledge of practically everything else, from Celtic ornaments to bone ship models. No less remarkable than the extent of his knowledge is the rapidity of his work; a few years ago I checked the output of a season and found that he had done about 3,500 lots [roughly twice that of other cataloguers]. He also finds time to be in the saleroom when anything important is on view, has innumerable interviews and sales at least one day almost every week. He is on friendly terms with very many collectors and museum officials, and most of the trade; a very high proportion of our business comes to us directly through him. His work accounts very largely for the steady growth of our works of art sales from 1924 to 1939.

What Hobson did not directly mention was Jim's enormous energy, his rigorous sense of order, his phenomenal memory, his speed of thought, his delightful courtesy, his integrity and the discipline he exacted from those who worked for him, without engendering anything except respect and affection. He virtually gave the whole of his life to Sotheby's, and for many people he personified the firm.

A transparent enamelled topographical beaker by Samuel Mohn and August Viertel, Dresden, 1812, height 3⅞in (9.8cm)
London £8,000 ($18,800). 3.XII.79

Notes on Contributors

Richard Barnett began his archaeological studies in 1930 at the British School of Archaeology in Athens. In 1932 he entered the British Museum and was Keeper of Western Asiatic Antiquities from 1955 to 1974. His publications include a *Catalogue of the Ivories from Nimrud in the British Museum* (1955); *Sculptures of Ashurpanipal* (1976) and *Ancient Ivories* (in press).

Wendy Baron is Curator of the Government Picture Collection and an authority on twentieth-century British art. She received her doctorate for her thesis on Sickert, on whom she subsequently published a monograph in 1973. She has researched and catalogued four major exhibitions of Sickert and his colleagues. Dr Baron has also published *Miss Ethel Sands and her Circle* (1977) and *The Camden Town Group* (1979).

Adelyn D. Breeskin is consultant to the National Collection of Fine Arts, Smithsonian Institution, Washington DC, on twentieth-century painting and sculpture. Mrs Breeskin is a specialist on the art of Mary Cassatt, and her publications include *The Graphic Work of Mary Cassatt* (1948, rev. 1970) and *Mary Cassatt: A Catalogue Raisonné of the Oils, Pastels, Watercolors and Drawings* (1980).

Martin Butlin is Keeper of the Historic British Collection at the Tate Gallery. He is joint author with Evelyn Joll of the complete catalogue of *The Paintings of J.M.W. Turner* (1977) and has compiled a catalogue raisonné of William Blake, to be published in 1981.

Simone Caudron is associated with a French government-sponsored project on medieval enamelling. Mme Caudron has written extensively on Limoges enamelling; her article on the Becket *châsse* in the *British Museum Yearbook* (1977) is a fundamental piece of research on the subject.

R.J. Charleston was Keeper of the Department of Ceramics and Glass at the Victoria and Albert Museum from 1963 until his retirement in 1976. He is President of the Glass Circle and editor of *Monographs on Glass*. His most recent publication is *A World History from the Corning Museum* (1980).

Philip J.C. Dark is an anthropologist, specialising in ethnic art, a subject that he has researched and taught in the United States and in Britain. His publications include *An Introduction to Benin Art and Technology* (1973); *Kilenge Art and Life: A look at a New Guinea People* (1974) and three parts of a thirty-two part study, *A Visual Ethnography of the Kilenge*.

David Hafler is an ardent collector of chess sets – an interest which led to his close friendship with the late John Harbeson. Mr Hafler has written articles on chessmen for several publications, and is an authority on the identification of pieces.

Frank Herrmann is a publisher and an author with a particular interest in the art market. He has written *The English as Collectors* (1972) and *Sotheby's: Portrait of an Auction House* (1980).

Jerry E. Patterson is a freelance writer on the art market. He was formerly contributing editor of *Art News*, and has worked for Sotheby's and Christie's in New York. Among his publications are *Autographs: a Collector's Guide* (1973) and *The City of New York, A History Illustrated from the Collections of the Museums of the City of New York* (1978).

Catherine Reynolds is a lecturer in the History of Art at the University of Reading. She is currently researching a PhD on fifteenth-century French painting.

Roy Strong is Director of the Victoria and Albert Museum. He is a specialist in the life and art of Tudor, Stuart and Victorian England. Among his recent publications are *The Cult of Elizabeth* (1977); *When did you last see your father? The Victorian Painter and British History* (1978) and *The Renaissance Garden in England* (1979).

Raymond Toole Stott has compiled the *Bibliography of English Conjuring* (1976, 1978) and, to date, four volumes of *Circus and Allied Arts* (1958–71), the former being dedicated to the late J.B. Findlay. Mr Toole Stott's own collection of circus memorabilia and Maughamiana is now in the University of California, Santa Barbara. He is a member of the Magic Circle.

Toby Falk and John Hayward are consultants to Sotheby Parke Bernet and the following contributors are experts at Sotheby Parke Bernet: Philippe Garner, Hilary Kay and James Miller (in London); William W. Stahl Jr and John Tancock (in New York).

Index